The
LOST ART
of
DISCIPLESHIP
Workbook

CONTENTS

CONTENTS

HOW TO READ THIS WORKBOOK

Welcome to *The Lost Art of Discipleship Workbook*! This workbook is designed to take you deeper into the truths and core values taught in *The Lost Art of Discipleship*. It is to be read in conjunction with *The Lost Art of Discipleship* book. My desire in creating this workbook is twofold:

- To empower you in your personal connection with the Lord.

- To encourage life-giving discussion and fellowship within the community, church, and family that God has placed you in.

To get the most out of this workbook, I recommend you sign up for *The Lost Art of Discipleship Online Course* and follow the lessons in conjunction with the respective chapters of the book.

SCAN ME! 📱

FOR PERSONAL STUDY:

After reading a chapter of *The Lost Art of Discipleship*, stop and take time to go through its corresponding chapter in this workbook. If you are also completing the online course, view the video for that chapter before continuing to the following one. My prayer is that every lesson will bring you into a greater revelation of the given topic. I believe that all of the provided information will become more than text on a page. I believe that you will be transformed by the renewing of your mind as you partner with the Holy Spirit in each chapter and walk out the activations in your daily life.

> *"Stop imitating the ideals and opinions of the culture around you, but be inwardly transformed by the Holy Spirit through a total reformation of how you think. This will empower you to discern God's will as you live a beautiful life, satisfying and perfect in his eyes."*
> -Romans 12:2 TPT

What you put into this workbook is what you will get out of it! It's not homework. It's about exploration, discovery, and having an ongoing conversation with the Holy Spirit.

Practically speaking, each chapter will present you with the opportunity to:

REVIEW the content from the chapter. REFLECT with the Holy Spirit on the truths and core values taught. Embrace the Word and BECOME your newfound revelations.

1. REVIEW *(Chapter Overview)*

A list of important points taken from their respective sections. This is just to jog your memory on the content you've already read.

2. REFLECT *(Going Deeper)*

To guide your time of reflection, you will be given a series of engaging and thought-provoking questions and prompts. Don't rush to answer! The purpose of this workbook is that these revelations will take root deep in your heart and mind.

> *"As water reflects the face, so one's life reflects the heart."*
> *-Proverbs 27:19 (NIV)*

The questions are here to turn your heart towards God for a time of intimate engagement with the Father, giving you a place to hear His voice! My prayer is that these questions will empower you to embrace the core values and implement them into your personal life. If you feel challenged by them, that is a good thing! You may also find it beneficial to revisit these questions over time, as adopting these core values into your own life will be a process.

It's important to note that self-initiated introspection and negative self-analysis is not the goal of this workbook. Rather, I pray that God's Spirit will lead you into a series of transformative revelations and experiences with Himself that will free you to be who He's designed you to be.

> *"It is written in the prophets, 'And they shall all be taught by God.' Therefore everyone who has heard and learned from the Father comes to Me."*
> *-John 6:45*

3. BECOME (*The Word Made Flesh*)

It's vital that you BECOME and manifest the core values by actively engaging with God's Word. At the end of each chapter, there will be a prompted Word Study to guide you deeper into knowing and cultivating the culture of God's Kingdom.

HOW TO DO A WORD STUDY:

When you finish a session you will be given the opportunity to dive into the Word of God. Studying individual passages of Scripture is a great way to break down seemingly big topics into bite-sized pieces. It will activate you in spending time in the Word, encountering God through Scripture, and learning directly from the Holy Spirit.

This workbook will assist you in your exploration of God's Word by highlighting key passages for you to read and meditate on. You are not limited to these Scriptures! I encourage you to use them as a springboard into a greater discovery of God's Word on the given subject.

Furthermore, as you go through the chapters, you will see different Activation Icons along the way. Each one is carefully placed to help you dive deeper into God's truth. If you see one of these icons, get ready for an activation!

ACTIVATION ICONS

MEDITATION

PRAYING IN TONGUES

DECLARATIONS

WHAT DOES IT MEAN TO MEDITATE?

"Blessed is the man who walks not in the counsel of the ungodly, nor stands in the path of sinners, nor sits in the seat of the scornful; but his delight is in the law of the Lord, and in His law he meditates day and night. He shall be like a tree planted by the rivers of water, that brings forth its fruit in its season, whose leaf also shall not wither; and whatever he does shall prosper."
-Psalm 1:1-3

The purpose of the Meditation sections is to give room for the Holy Spirit to minister truth to you in a personal and intimate way. As you learn with your mind and intellect, it's also vital that you receive and adopt the core values into your heart. Meditation is simple. Many have seen it in a skewed light and associate it with pagan beliefs. However, meditation is absolutely biblical! Many religions have taken meditation and taught that its purpose is to empty your mind from the worries of life. But the Word of God says that the "truth" sets you free, and we experience freedom as we receive His truth and allow it to fill our hearts and minds. True meditation is filling your mind with the truth and reality of Jesus Christ.

Through meditation, we commune with God and allow the Scriptures to direct conversation with Him. When you meditate, fix your mind on Jesus. Chew on the specific passages by reading them multiple times, all the while letting the Holy Spirit transform the way you think. Meditating is like conversing with God about Scripture. You are coming to God's Word to meet Him and get to know Him, and He wants to reveal Himself to you. You may sense that God wants to show you how this verse applies to an area of your life, and perhaps other Scriptures may come to mind. The objective is continual, conscious communion with Christ, so eventually, you may move beyond conscious thought about the Scripture itself. Anytime you feel your mind wander from the subject, simply revisit the Bible verse to steer your thoughts back to Jesus.

"Finally, brethren, whatever things are true, whatever things are noble, whatever things are just, whatever things are pure, whatever things are lovely, whatever things are of good report, if there is any virtue and if there is anything praiseworthy—meditate on these things."
-Philippians 4:8

WHAT DOES IT MEAN TO PRAY IN TONGUES?

"Pursue love, and desire spiritual gifts, but especially that you may prophesy. For he who speaks in a tongue does not speak to men but to God, for no one understands him; however, in the spirit he speaks mysteries. But he who prophesies speaks edification and exhortation and comfort to men. He who speaks in a tongue edifies himself, but he who prophesies edifies the church."
-1 Corinthians 14:1-4

When the Spirit of God came upon the disciples in Acts 2, they were all overshadowed with tongues of fire (see verses 1-4). Paul later describes praying in tongues as speaking mysteries that edify and build you up. That's the purpose of this Discipleship Activation: to allow the Spirit of God to do all the talking! As you partner with Him in this, the truths you are learning will sink deeper and faster into your mind and heart than they ever could by your own willpower. This activation will give you a subject or topic to keep in mind as you speak in tongues and allow the Lord to do what only He can do.

"But you, beloved, building yourselves up on your most holy faith, praying in the Holy Spirit, keep yourselves in the love of God, looking for the mercy of our Lord Jesus Christ unto eternal life."
-Jude 20-21

WHAT ARE DECLARATIONS?

"Death and life are in the power of the tongue, and those who love it will eat its fruit."
-Proverbs 18:21

Declaring the truth trains us to use our voice to implement God's Word in our lives. Speaking His truth about who we are establishes us in it by renewing our minds, allowing us to see His reality become our own. When you hear yourself speaking the truth with boldness, it creates faith and allows you to partner with the reality you're releasing.

Paul exhorts us in Romans 12:2, "Do not conform to the pattern of this world, but be transformed by the renewing of your mind." Our transformation comes when our minds are renewed as we declare God's truth, speak in faith, and believe who we are in Christ.

John 8:32 says, "And you shall know the truth, and the truth shall make you free." Making declarations doesn't set us free—knowing the truth does! By speaking the truth regularly, we start to believe more deeply what God says about us. God's Word promises us that when we abide in His truth, we will start to believe it wholeheartedly as His Word begins to renew our minds. As you verbalize the provided declarations throughout this workbook, trust that God is establishing every word into your heart and mind.

"I believed, therefore I spoke..."
-Psalm 116:10

SELF-ASSESSMENT

At the end of each chapter, the self-assessment section is designed to help you evaluate your growth. If you find it helpful, complete these sections and revisit them over time to see how you have grown in each area.

FOR TEACHING OR LEADING A GROUP:

At the end of the workbook, I have included a list of questions to help you lead and conduct your own *Lost Art of Discipleship* Bible study or homegroup. I believe God is raising fathers and mothers all over the planet to empower the future generations of sons and daughters. I pray this workbook would be a beautiful springboard for you and your group to become everything God intends.

PART ONE

POSITION YOURSELF AS A SON OR DAUGHTER

CHAPTER ONE

DISCIPLESHIP AT ITS ROOTS

Discipleship is more than good advice at home groups or Sunday services. It is a means of being conformed to the very image and likeness of Christ, entirely by relationship. To be a disciple is to live in close association with someone whom you wish to model your life after. In the days of the early church, how did they recognize the disciples of Jesus? It was through the way His followers loved one another. Everyone knew those who followed Him because those who did acted just like Him. To be a disciple is not about modeling ourselves after a man—it's about modeling ourselves after the Son of Man. When you rest in and imitate the light coming from a father or mother and when you grab hold of it as your own, that is discipleship.

OVERVIEW

- Discipleship is God's idea! Long-lasting transformation comes from making disciples.

- The Gospel is designed to change us from the inside-out. The more the internal world of the believer is glowing with God's light, the more we will see the world around us covered in the knowledge of His glory.

- The terms "spiritual father" and "spiritual mother" should not be dirty words! Healthy fathers and mothers naturally model noble character and a walk with God for sons/daughters to emulate.

- Submission is not about controlling people. It's about empowering them.

- Discipleship starts in one of three ways:
    a) God ordains it.
    b) You choose it.
    c) They choose it.

- Everyone needs a "Paul", a "Barnabas", and a "Timothy" (a father/mother, a close friend, and a son/daughter to pour into).

- Pray and look for a father or mother that genuinely knows the Lord and is rooted in God's Word. Review the chapter for more specific pointers!

GOING DEEPER

Discipleship is God's design for world transformation. The Lord has an incredible plan for you on this journey of discipleship.

1. What has your experience been like with leaders in your life? What negative experiences have you had? What positive experiences have you had? Be open and honest with God as you reflect.

_____

_____

_____

_____

_____

_____

_____

2. Based on your personal experience and what you have read, what are some characteristics of godly leaders? How should they carry themselves? How should they treat those they lead?

_____

_____

_____

_____

_____

_____

3. If you've had a bad experience with a leader, take time to talk through it with the Lord. On the lines below,

- Write down the name of the person that wronged you and any details of the experience as you feel led.

- Choose to forgive the person that wronged you, writing a prayer of forgiveness.

- Ask God for His perspective of this person and add a blessing to the end of your prayer.

4. List 3 areas you would like to grow in through the course of *The Lost Art of Discipleship Workbook*. Be as descriptive, detailed, and specific as possible. As you move forward with this course, it will be very helpful to keep these goals in mind.

SCAN ME!

THE WORD MADE FLESH

It's time to dive heart-first into the Word of God. It's one thing to know about a truth intellectually, but it's another thing entirely to become it! Just as Jesus Christ was the embodiment of the Word, we are called to embody and manifest the Scriptures in every area of our lives.

WORD STUDY

Check out the following passages on discipleship. No matter how familiar you may be with these verses, ask the Lord to emphasize the weight and value each of them carries for you *today*.

> Matthew 28:16-20
> John 8:31-32
> Luke 6:40
> 2 Timothy 2:2

What mindsets do you see God shifting in you as you read these Scriptures? Are there any core concepts about discipleship that are sticking out to you as you read? Write what God speaks to you on the lines below.

CHAPTER TWO

HUMILITY

Humility is a heart posture that makes discipleship possible and leads to growth and transformation. It's not a grand show of lowliness. It's an internal world that has given up its right to be in control and taken on a willingness to be taught.

SURRENDER + SUBMISSION = HUMILITY

HUMILITY AT A GLANCE

The most foundational aspect of discipleship is humility. A teachable heart leaves room for the input of fathers and mothers.

Surrendering to God first and foremost puts His guidance at the center of our lives. When we surrender to His will and trust in His voice, we will automatically find that submission to spiritual leaders comes naturally. Why? Because our trust isn't rooted in a natural man or woman but a supernatural God!

True submission is built on this kind of trust, not on fear or control. It starts with an open and humble heart which allows issues beyond our awareness to be addressed and removed. Being a son or a daughter starts exactly there—on the altar of humility.

SURRENDER

Surrender is the entryway to the power and character of Jesus Christ.

OVERVIEW:

Everything starts with surrender. When your heart is yielded to God's voice, your life will be led into limitless possibilities.

- Surrender is the first step of discipleship.

- True surrender is not outward, but inward. It is a matter of the heart, not just a physical display of obedience. It's putting your trust in God above all else, and that heart of surrender leads to true obedience.

- Surrender grows stronger the more you understand that God is good and that He is for you. We naturally surrender when we know and experience His love.

- Trusting leaders is ultimately a reflection of the choice to trust God. We trust our leaders, confident that they are God's instruments to raise us up in Him.

- Discipleship is God's idea. When we surrender to God, we surrender to His game-plan for changing the world.

- God is the ultimate supplier. The more you have, the more you get to choose to trust Him beyond anything you might consider to be a worldly advantage.

> "
> THEREFORE I URGE YOU, BRETHREN, BY THE MERCIES OF GOD, TO PRESENT YOUR BODIES A LIVING AND HOLY SACRIFICE, ACCEPTABLE TO GOD, WHICH IS YOUR SPIRITUAL SERVICE OF WORSHIP.
>
> **ROMANS 12:1 NASB**

NOTES:

_____

_____

_____

_____

MEDITATION

Take time to read Ezekiel 47:1-6. After reading it, spend a few minutes in meditation. See yourself as Ezekiel at the bank of the river of the Spirit. Go ankle-deep, knee-deep, waist-deep, and finally beyond what you could possibly cross on your own. The deeper you go, the less control you have. As you continue to go deeper, another layer of surrender unfolds.

_____

_____

_____

_____

_____

_____

_____

_____

_____

GOING DEEPER

We could all go deeper in surrender to God. Like Ezekiel in the waters that flowed from the temple, all of us could wander further into the currents of God's grace: ankle-deep, knee-deep, waist-deep, and finally, in over our heads.

1. What are some specific areas of your life that you've already chosen to surrender to God, and in which you have resolved to follow Him no matter what?

2. What have been the hardest things to surrender? Ask the Holy Spirit why and write what He reveals to you.

3. What fruit have you seen as a result of giving these things into God's hands?

4. Take some time to pray and ask God if there are any areas of your life you haven't fully surrendered to Him. Don't spend your time "dumpster diving," looking for all the bad in your life, but rather invite God in and allow Him to draw your heart into a deeper level of surrender. Write a prayer of surrender, opening your heart to God as He speaks and ministers truth to you.

_____

_____

_____

_____

5. Now, give Him everything you've been holding on to. Let it go! If there's something you're having trouble giving over, take extra time to ask Him why it's so difficult to release it. Ask Him for His grace to surrender—you can't do it in your strength! As you open your heart and lay yourself on God's altar, ask Him what lies at the end of surrender. Just as Jesus suffered for the joy set before Him, what is the joy set before you as you give it all to the King of kings? Write what you hear and feel.

_____

_____

_____

_____

SCAN ME!

NOTES:

SUBMISSION

Submission relinquishes your need to be in control. It allows you to lay your life down in total trust and dependence on God.

OVERVIEW:

- Submission is a fundamental truth that everyone should grasp. In order to be a father or mother, you must first be a son or daughter.

- Submission is the fruit of surrendering to God.

- The lens through which you view God will dictate how you respond when you receive direction from authorities in your life.

- The goal of submission is to raise sons and daughters who are internally governed by the Holy Spirit.

- Submission says, "I'm going to trust you more than I trust myself because I trust that God has put you in my life for such a time as this. You have something (maturity, wisdom, revelation) that I need."

- Submission and trust are revealed not only in what we do but in the motivations and heart posture under the surface.

- When you trust God to direct your steps you will naturally trust the leaders He puts in your life.

- Trusting in leadership leads to growth and longevity.

> "
> OBEY YOUR LEADERS AND SUBMIT TO THEM, FOR THEY ARE KEEPING WATCH OVER YOUR SOULS, AS THOSE WHO WILL HAVE TO GIVE AN ACCOUNT. LET THEM DO THIS WITH JOY AND NOT WITH GROANING, FOR THAT WOULD BE OF NO ADVANTAGE TO YOU.
>
> HEBREWS 13:17

GOING DEEPER

Spiritual submission allows us to accurately represent the Father to a fatherless world. We aren't made for independence. We are made for relationships full of both honor and humility.

1. What is your natural response when you hear the word "submit"?

2. What does worldly, unbiblical submission look like?

3. What would pure, biblical submission look like to you?

4. What do you think would be the potential benefits of living a submitted life? What are the benefits of having someone you're accountable to?

_____

_____

_____

_____

_____

_____

_____

_____

_____

_____

_____

_____

THE WORD MADE FLESH

 WORD STUDY

Dive into the Word and read Genesis 22:1-14. As you read it, meditate on what it would have been like to be Isaac. See yourself going up the mountain with your father, Abraham. See yourself getting on the altar in total trust and abandonment. What would it have been like for Isaac? What would have been going through his head?

_____

_____

_____

_____

_____

_____

Now, take time to read the following Scriptures on submission. Ask the Lord to breathe on each passage. Let these verses springboard you into a greater and deeper revelation of what it means to be a submitted son or daughter!

Hebrews 13:7, 17

1 Peter 5:5-7

1 Corinthians 4:14-17, 11:1

Ephesians 5:21

SELF-ASSESSMENT

Take time to reflect on what humility currently looks like in your life. Do you feel you have a strong understanding of submission and surrender? Or do you feel it's something you can grow in? No matter where you are at, God's Spirit is ready and waiting to empower you to new heights. God will never put you down, He will only work to transform you and lift you up!

Rate yourself in the respective areas, 1 meaning you really need to work on it, and 5 meaning you are thriving in this area of life.

Where do I see myself in this area?

1   2   3   4   5

Where do my friends see me in this area?

1   2   3   4   5

Where does my family see me in this area?

1   2   3   4   5

Where do my leaders see me in this area?

1   2   3   4   5

After the assessment, how do you feel? Write a few thoughts below. Share your ideas and/or thoughts and ask for advice, wisdom, and guidance on how to further develop yourself in this area.

_____

_____

_____

_____

"HUMILITY IS NOT THINKING LESS OF YOURSELF, IT'S THINKING OF YOURSELF LESS."

- C. S. LEWIS

CHAPTER THREE

RELATIONSHIP

In God's world, relationships advance the kingdom.

Discipleship at its foundation is a relationship. It's an empowering and intimate connection between a spiritual father/mother and a spiritual son/daughter.

PURSUING LEADERSHIP + INTENTIONALITY + SERVANTHOOD = RELATIONSHIP

A discipled relationship is one built on mutual love and trust.

While sons and daughters are often pursued by fathers and mothers, relationships are a two-way street, and intentional pursuit must be reciprocated.

We pursue leaders because we want to grow into the likeness of who Jesus is. This pursuit is one full of honor and trust, knowing that God has placed them in your life for such a time as this. This intentional pursuit unlocks exponential growth for us because as we express love and give honor to our leaders the connection deepens and the transformation quickens.

Out of this connection comes a genuine heart to serve. Those who serve seek to selflessly love, understanding that their actions are ultimately worship unto the Lord, fueled by His love and empowered by His grace. Now that's a recipe for a strong relationship!

PURSUING LEADERSHIP

Pursuit is honor on display. You will never pursue what you don't honor.

OVERVIEW:

Every relationship is two-sided. Without intentionally pursuing another person, relational growth will decelerate.

- Sonship begins when a son/daughter pursues a leader in a real, authentic relationship.

- We are called to imitate our lives after others. "Imitate me just as I also imitate Christ" (1 Cor. 1:11 NASB).

- Pursuit leads to transformation.

- How people view and treat their leaders often reveals their perspective of and relationship with God.

- One of the biggest things you can do in your pursuit of leaders is deciding how you are going to view them.

- A practical way to pursue is by asking questions. The people who ask the most questions grow the most.

- Invite leaders into your life. Allow them to see the good, the bad, and the ugly.

> "
> ENTREAT ME NOT TO LEAVE YOU, OR TO TURN BACK FROM FOLLOWING AFTER YOU; FOR WHEREVER YOU GO, I WILL GO; AND WHEREVER YOU LODGE, I WILL LODGE; YOUR PEOPLE SHALL BE MY PEOPLE, AND YOUR GOD, MY GOD.
>
> **RUTH 1:16**

NOTES:

_____

_____

_____

_____

GOING DEEPER

1. Write down the name(s) of someone you know (a mother/father figure) that you admire, trust, and feel you could learn from.

_____

_____

_____

2. Pray and ask God how you can intentionally pursue the leaders He's emphasized to you. Write their name below. What does it look like to intentionally pursue this particular leader?

_____

_____

_____

3. Set up a meeting and connect with one leader you feel led to pursue as a spiritual father or mother. Let them know that you would love to learn from them, and ask if they would be willing to get together on a regular basis. Use the space below to brainstorm questions you would like to ask them/what you want to learn from his or her life.

_____

_____

_____

_____

4. If you're finding the idea of pursuing a father or mother difficult, take time to ask God if there is any belief you have toward leadership that is limiting you. No matter what walls or objections you may feel, surrender it to God and allow Him to minister truth to your heart and mind. Journal your thoughts and God's responses here.

"God, I let go of any beliefs about leaders from the past that may be limiting me and I invite you to renew my mind as I go through *The Lost Art of Discipleship*."

NOTES:

_____

_____

_____

_____

_____

_____

INTENTIONALITY

Deep, loving relationships are not established on accident. They are *intentional*. They are created and developed on purpose.

OVERVIEW:

Intentionality brings relationships to life...

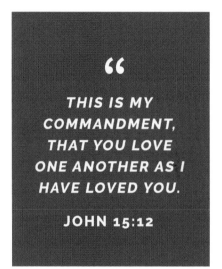

> **THIS IS MY COMMANDMENT, THAT YOU LOVE ONE ANOTHER AS I HAVE LOVED YOU.**
>
> **JOHN 15:12**

- "You can have a certain level of relationship without intentionality, but a relationship will need intentionality to thrive."

- If intentionality is not reciprocated to your leaders then the full cycle of love is incomplete.

- The foundation of intentionality is selflessness. It flows from love, not obligation.

- The more you invest in the relationship as a son or daughter, the more you will receive from your leaders.

- The reward of a deep relationship far outweighs the potential time and effort of intentionality.

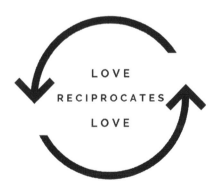

LOVE
RECIPROCATES
LOVE

Important note: If you're still finding it hard to connect with a leader, don't worry! You're not alone. God will lead and direct you as you yield to His plan for your life. If you're still in a position of not having a father or mother figure in mind to pursue, then take time again to review the section on Pursuing Leadership. I would recommend you build a relationship with a leader through the remainder of this workbook.

GOING DEEPER

1. What are some ways you have seen intentionality displayed, whether in your life or the life of another?

_____

_____

_____

_____

2. What was the result of that (those) intentional act(s)? How did you notice it affect the person on the receiving end?

_____

_____

_____

_____

3. What intentional acts would make you feel loved and thought of? Write down a list of different things that would greatly bless you if done for you.

_____

_____

_____

_____

4. What intentional acts would you like to do for the people around you? Dream big, think outside the box, don't mind the money in your account as much as the love you have for the person (people). Write a few ideas below.

_____

_____

_____

_____

5. Choose an intentional act from your list and do it this week for someone you look up to/your spiritual leader. Write the who and what below.

_____

_____

_____

_____

Keep a note of the things you notice friends, family, and leaders appreciate. Remember that little things can make a big difference in the lives of those around you. Don't lose heart thinking that something intentional has to be extravagantly expensive or impressively original. Simple acts of intentionality go a long way!

PRAY IN TONGUES

God is more intentional than you and I could ever be! When we pray in the Spirit, we tap into God's storehouse of love and intentionality.

The Lord knows everyone so specifically and with so much detail. He knows exactly what makes a person go crazy with joy.

Right now, fix your mind on a person you really love and want to bless. As you think of that person, begin to pray in tongues with the intention of discovering God's heart for them. Take time doing this and allow God to speak to you about what that person would really like and appreciate from you. Write down what He speaks when He speaks it, and all the while continue to pray in the Spirit. Expect to hear Him vividly and clearly!

NOTES:

_____

_____

_____

_____

_____

SERVANTHOOD

Servanthood... it's not about you! Let go of your own interests and look to serve those around you.

OVERVIEW:

Servanthood is a labor of love that communicates honor and respect within a relationship.

- It's not about you!

- From the overflow of Jesus' relationship with the Father, He was able to look to others before Himself.

- We serve best when our focus is on God and not ourselves.

- Serve from your heart. When you love someone it is only natural to serve them.

- Jesus is our role model for servanthood.

- Serving out of obligation leads to burning out.

- Look to fill the gaps. There are always ways you can serve.

- Servanthood leads to a deeper connection.

> "
>
> FOR YOU, BRETHREN, HAVE BEEN CALLED TO LIBERTY; ONLY DO NOT USE LIBERTY AS AN OPPORTUNITY FOR THE FLESH, BUT THROUGH LOVE SERVE ONE ANOTHER.
>
> **GALATIANS 5:13**

GOING DEEPER

1. From your own experience, have you noticed a difference between serving from love and serving for love?

_____

_____

_____

_____

2. What are some ways you've seen servanthood make a difference? How have you seen it impact someone's life?

_____

_____

_____

_____

3. What are some ways you've served? How did it affect the person you were serving?

_____

_____

_____

_____

SCAN ME!

5. What are some practical ways you can serve...

Your family?

_____

_____

Your friends?

_____

_____

Your church?

_____

_____

Your workplace?

_____

_____

6. Take action and do it! Choose a person or a place to serve in a way you never have before. Record your experience below!

_____

_____

_____

_____

_____

_____

THE WORD MADE FLESH

 WORD STUDY

Read the following two passages: Deuteronomy 21:17 and 2 Kings 2:1-15.

In the Old Testament, the double portion was preserved for the firstborn son. Elisha wasn't merely hunting for an anointing, he was pursuing sonship. Now, put yourself in the shoes of Elisha. Perceive and take ownership of the value of pursuing and receiving from a leader. It is not a pursuit of flesh and blood, it is a spiritual pursuit of blessing and inheritance. Where else in Scripture do you see the power of pursuit on display? Dive into the Word and discover more on this subject. Allow the Lord to guide and teach you! Write your discoveries below:

_____

_____

_____

_____

_____

_____

SELF-ASSESSMENT

Take time to reflect on what your relationship with leaders looks like. Do you feel like you understand what it means to pursue, serve, and be intentional? Or are you still working to discover what all of that really means? No matter where you are at, God's Spirit is ready and waiting to empower you to new heights. God will never put you down, He will only work to transform you and lift you up!

Rate yourself in the respective areas, 1 meaning you really need to work on it, and 5 meaning you are thriving in this area of life.

Where do I see myself in this area?

1   2   3   4   5

Where do my friends see me in this area?

1   2   3   4   5

Where does my family see me in this area?

1   2   3   4   5

Where do my leaders see me in this area?

1   2   3   4   5

After the assessment, how do you feel? Write a few thoughts below. Share your ideas and/or thoughts and ask for advice, wisdom, and guidance on how to further develop yourself in this area.

_____

_____

_____

_____

"CHRISTIANITY IS NOT A RELIGION OR A PHILOSOPHY, BUT A RELATIONSHIP & A LIFESTYLE."

- RICK WARREN

CHAPTER FOUR

GROWTH

The focus of growth is not behavior modification but rather inward heart transformation.

The purpose of discipleship is found in seeing sons and daughters grow into the image and likeness of Jesus Christ.

CONFRONTATION • INTEGRITY • RESPONSIBILITY = GROWTH

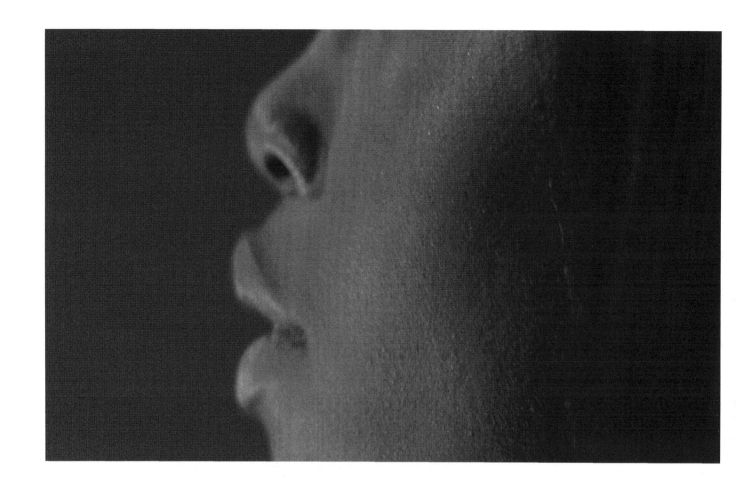

GROWTH AT A GLANCE

Growth comes from the inside-out. We cannot simply modify our behavior in order to grow; we must start by developing key values and beliefs within that will result in true transformation.

Integrity is an essential core value that serves as a guide for our actions, and it is built in the moment-by-moment, day-to-day. Motivated by love for God and others, we grow in integrity by following through with our words and doing what we know is honorable, even when no one is looking, it is inconvenient, or it seems insignificant.

We must partner with the Holy Spirit in His guidance through the conscience in every choice we make.

Responsibility will strengthen this foundation of character and help us grow in influence with others as they see our reliability.

Humility ensures that we will be open to confrontation, trusting that it comes from love and is necessary for our growth.

Avoiding judgement will ensure we do not miss out on an opportunity to grow. Though these values may seem rudimentary, being firmly established in character is the key to true growth as a son or daughter.

CONFRONTATION

Don't hide from the truth. Allow lies, insecurities, and misconceptions to be *confronted*. The truth is a light that opens the eyes of the blind.

OVERVIEW:

Sometimes, love looks like confrontation...

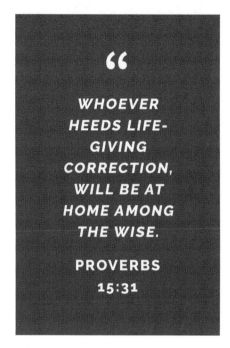

"
WHOEVER HEEDS LIFE-GIVING CORRECTION, WILL BE AT HOME AMONG THE WISE.

PROVERBS 15:31

- "Confrontation" shouldn't be a scary word!

- The goal of confrontation should always be deeper levels of connection and growth.

- Love should always be the motive and foundation of confrontation.

- If we don't understand the heart of confrontation, we will always be afraid of it.

- We should embrace confrontation because it will lead to inward heart transformation.

- Confrontation allows others to speak into your blind spots. When truth exposes something in your heart, grace comes to transform it.

- When confronted for something you've done wrong, remember the 5 A's of cleaning up a mess: Admit, Apologize, Ask for forgiveness, Acknowledge how you will change, and Appreciate the other person for confronting you.

THE 5 A'S OF CLEANING UP A MESS

1. Admit you are wrong
2. Apologize
3. Ask for forgiveness
4. Acknowledge how you will change
5. Appreciate the confrontation

GOING DEEPER

1. How do you feel about confrontation? What emotions arise when you think about confronting others or being confronted by someone?

2. How do you think confrontation will be beneficial in your life?

3. Is there anyone in your life who is willing to lovingly confront you? Ask a leader you respect to confront you and give you feedback more regularly. Explain to them that you want to grow and that their advice is valuable and important to you.

4. Are there things within your own family, workplace, or friend group that you would like to see change? If so, what are they, and how could you lovingly confront these issues?

_____

_____

_____

_____

5. Don't hesitate! Talk to a leader in your life about these issues and let them know your game plan for confronting these situations. Write down the outcome below.

_____

_____

_____

_____

INTEGRITY

Integrity makes us whole. Without it, we are divided, indifferent, and powerless.

OVERVIEW:

Integrity is a key ingredient for consistent long-term growth.

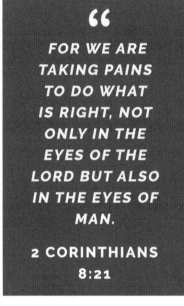

- Integrity is doing what is just and right, even when no one is looking.

- The foundation of your life should be built with integrity, not compromise.

- Integrity is a byproduct of loving the Lord and others.

- Integrity begins with the way we think and works its way into our daily lives.

- Integrity is a self-working mechanism that sustains growth.

- Integrity keeps its word. "Let your 'yes' be 'yes' and your 'no' be 'no'" (Matt. 5:37).

- Live from your convictions no matter how significant or insignificant the situation may appear.

- Integrity is formed in the shadows but revealed in the spotlight. The more you say "yes" to God in the secret, the more you will clearly display His character to others in day-to-day circumstances.

NOTES:

_____

_____

_____

_____

GOING DEEPER

1. Write down a list of people (that you know or know of) that walk in integrity. Choose 2 names. What is the result of this core value being practiced in their lives?

2. What is an area of your life that you feel integrous, secure, and consistent in (an area without compromise)? What has been the result of such integrity in this area of your life?

3. Now, reflect on what areas you feel could use an "integrity upgrade." Write down your thoughts below:

4. Give these areas to God and ask Him to help you walk in integrity. Ask the Lord to give you practical steps that will empower you to walk with integrity in the areas you just listed. Write what He shares with you.

 **DECLARATIONS**

Integrity starts with a choice. When your mind has resolved to remain steadfast in its convictions, you will glow with integrity. Make these declarations and partner with truth *now*. Don't wait for temptations to arise to make up your mind. Know in your heart today who you are and what you will choose. Make these declarations (as many times as you'd like) out loud and with boldness:

I am loved by God! He chose to give His only Son in exchange for my life!

I am an oak of righteousness!

God lives inside of me! His nature radiates in and through my being!

I am a new creation in Christ!

His blood has washed every part of me, from the top of my head to the tip of my toes!

I am holy because He is holy! My holiness doesn't come from my flesh; it comes from God's Spirit!

I will never again be a slave to sin! Jesus has set me free—forever!

SCAN ME!

NOTES:

RESPONSIBILITY

Responsibility is the stewardship of who you are, what you do, and how you do it.

OVERVIEW:

Responsibility is necessary for growth, progression, and influence.

- Growing in responsibility starts with the small, everyday tasks. How we handle these tasks reveals how we are stewarding the vision God has given us.

- If you are responsible with what God has given you, He will entrust you with more.

- Responsible people are good stewards of their own hearts. Maintaining an internal attitude and posture of Christlikeness is our greatest responsibility.

- Take responsibility for your actions and own up to your mistakes.

- Steward what's put in front of you no matter how small or insignificant it may seem. This will open doors of influence as you continue to grow.

- Growth can be measured by the size of the responsibilities you can take on.

- In the midst of your responsibilities, don't lose sight of the bigger picture; it's all about love and it's all about Him!

> "
> HE WHO IS FAITHFUL IN WHAT IS LEAST IS FAITHFUL ALSO IN MUCH; AND HE WHO IS UNJUST IN WHAT IS LEAST IS UNJUST ALSO IN MUCH.
>
> LUKE 16:10

GOING DEEPER

1. Who are some of the most responsible people you know? How have you seen this core value positively impact their lives?

2. What are some examples of things you have stewarded well? What's been the benefit of your mature responsibility in these areas?

3. Is there anything in your life that you feel you could steward better? If so, how could you grow in responsibility?

4. Ask a leader for feedback! Ask them how they perceive your ability to steward things. Ask them tough questions: "Do you feel I'm at a level of maturity yet to handle a small task or project for you? If not, how can I get there? If I am, how can I continue to grow in responsibility?"

THE WORD MADE FLESH

WORD STUDY

As you read in *The Lost Art of Discipleship*, the Bible is riddled with Scriptures on confrontation, instruction, and correction. Now it's not just the Old Testament that talks about it; Jesus also corrected His disciples frequently. God is love and, sometimes, love looks like confrontation. Read the following passage and ask the Holy Spirit to reveal the heart of Christ. How many times does Jesus bring correction or instruction to His disciples in this passage? What do you think His heart was for each situation?

Luke 9:37-56

SELF-ASSESSMENT

Take time to reflect on what growth currently looks like in your life. Is it something you run from or towards? Where are you at with confrontation, integrity, and responsibility? How can you grow in these areas? No matter where you are at, God's Spirit is ready and waiting to empower you to new heights. God will never put you down, He will only work to transform you and lift you up!

Rate yourself in the respective areas, 1 meaning you really need to work on it, and 5 meaning you are thriving in this area of life.

Where do I see myself in this area?

1   2   3   4   5

Where do my friends see me in this area?

1   2   3   4   5

Where does my family see me in this area?

1   2   3   4   5

Where do my leaders see me in this area?

1   2   3   4   5

After the assessment, how do you feel? Write a few thoughts below. Share your ideas and/or thoughts and ask for advice, wisdom, and guidance on how to further develop yourself in this area.

_____

_____

_____

_____

"GROWTH SHOULD BE MORE IMPORTANT THAN OUR DESIRE TO REMAIN COMFORTABLE."

- THE LOST ART OF DISCIPLESHIP

PART TWO

LEAD AS A FATHER OR MOTHER

We are all called to greatness, but greatness cannot end in ourselves; it must stretch far beyond our reach and ripple through the lives of those we lead.

Before you continue!

How have you been empowered to position yourself as a son or daughter? Do you feel you're ready to begin pouring into a "Timothy"? If not, don't worry! You're probably more ready than you think! Connect with a leader, ask questions, and learn more about how to prepare yourself to be a mentor. If you're ready to go, begin to establish a discipled connection with someone you know you can offer wisdom to.

LOVE

Love is the greatest reality we can live by.

As a father or mother, love is invaluable. Love is the key ingredient to discipleship. Without it, nothing would happen—just powerless religion.

BELIEF + SERVANTHOOD = LOVE

LOVE AT A GLANCE

Selfless love is the cornerstone of the father/son and mother/daughter relationship.

When we lay our lives down in love, we see the grace of God transform people supernaturally.

This love is expressed through belief: encouraging people to reach a potential they may see themselves incapable of reaching. Lovingly communicating belief unlocks hidden potential in those we lead, setting them free from lies they believe about themselves.

Servanthood is a true mark of selfless love. Leaders who love selflessly understand that promotion allows for more opportunities to serve. Selfless leaders are willing to pour into their sons and daughters, relying on the love of God to give even when it isn't easy.

SCAN ME! 📱

BELIEF

Belief is the backing force behind transformation.

OVERVIEW:

Belief gives you vision for discipleship no matter the storm, the circumstance, or the misunderstanding.

- If sons and daughters know they are believed in, they will have confidence no matter what obstacle comes their way.

- Believing in those you lead positions you to have influence in their lives.

- God's perception of us remains consistently good despite what we believe about ourselves.

- Discipleship requires you to see those you lead in light of who they are in Christ and to believe in their fullest potential.

- Belief is a proactive championing, not a passive attitude.

- The more you believe in who your sons and daughters are, the easier it will be to confront them when they are out of line with their identity.

- It is important to champion your sons and daughters in private, in front of their friends, and in front of people they've never met.

> "
> THEREFORE ENCOURAGE ONE ANOTHER AND BUILD UP ONE ANOTHER, JUST AS YOU ALSO ARE DOING.
>
> 1 THESSALONIANS 5:11

NOTES:

_____

_____

_____

_____

_____

GOING DEEPER

1. There are many movies with a prominent father or mother figure that display the power of discipleship, such as *The Karate Kid*. These movies have a mentor figure who helps the hero accomplish his or her goal. Pick a favorite movie and identify a mentor figure. Write how the mentor figure's influence impacted the life of the character he or she poured into. What did the son or daughter figure learn? What was he or she able to accomplish because of that leader's investment that they did not believe was possible before?

_____

_____

_____

_____

2. Take time to connect with a leader in your life and ask them what they believe you're capable of. Ask them to call out your true potential in Christ. Write what they say below.

_____

_____

_____

_____

3. How can you take hold of your full potential? Pray and ask God for an action plan. Share what you hear with a leader, and write his or her comments and encouragement below.

_____

_____

_____

_____

4. Now, take this to those you are leading! Write down a few names of people you believe are capable of much more than their current mindsets allow. (If you are not currently mentoring anyone, take time to ask God who He is leading you to pour into. Write their names below.)

_____

_____

_____

_____

5. How can you display your belief in these people? How can you encourage them to step into what they're made to do?

_____

_____

_____

_____

_____

6. DO IT!

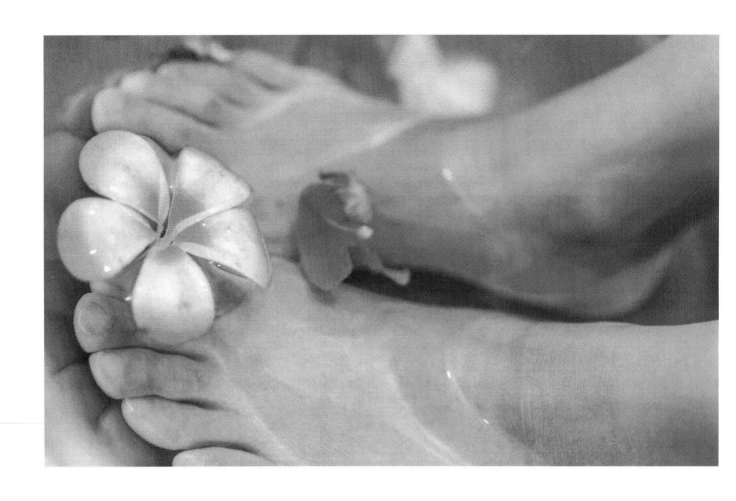

NOTES:

SERVANTHOOD

True leaders are those who have been upgraded into a higher capacity of *serving* those around them.

OVERVIEW:

Servanthood should not be bypassed by a position of leadership. True leaders embrace servanthood daily.

- Servanthood is a direct manifestation of a heart consumed with love.

- Serving and loving people is a choice. You are not a victim to the people around you; you *choose* to be a servant.

- Jesus is the ultimate example of a leader, and He demonstrated servanthood in everything He did.

- Great leaders view leadership as an access point to even greater ways to serve humanity.

- You are not leading because you want a title; you are leading because you want to love and serve those around you.

- Servanthood is an act of selfless love that prioritizes others above your own convenience.

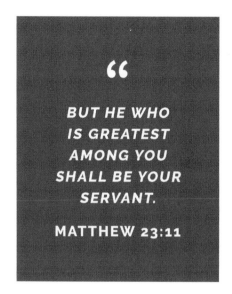

"

BUT HE WHO IS GREATEST AMONG YOU SHALL BE YOUR SERVANT.

MATTHEW 23:11

GOING DEEPER

1. Who is someone you know of who is an authentic, "from the heart" servant? How do you see them affecting the people around them? How do you think modeling servanthood will lead to a value for serving in those you lead?

_____

_____

_____

_____

2. If you are in a position of leadership, what are some ways you could serve those you are leading? How could you practically bless them and take some of the load off of their shoulders?

_____

_____

_____

_____

3. How do you think having a community of people who serve one another would affect your church or organization's culture? How about your city?

_____

_____

_____

_____

4. Write down some practical ways you can serve those you interact with regularly. What would they appreciate from you?

_____

_____

_____

_____

5. Serve someone this week! Do something out of the ordinary and expect an extraordinary result. Write down what happens below.

_____

_____

_____

_____

_____

_____

THE WORD MADE FLESH

WORD STUDY

Read John 13:1-17. Jesus' belief in His disciples empowered Him to serve them. He did not see them as a bunch of "Average Joes." He saw them as chosen vessels that were made to change the world. Where else in the Bible do you see someone's belief in another person empower them to serve?

_____

_____

_____

_____

_____

_____

SELF-ASSESSMENT

Take time to reflect on what love currently looks like in your life. Do you feel like you believe in and serve those you are leading well? Or do you feel it's something you can grow in? No matter where you are at, God's Spirit is ready and waiting to empower you to new heights. God will never put you down, He will only work to transform you and lift you up!

Rate yourself in the respective areas, 1 meaning you really need to work on it, and 5 meaning you are thriving in this area of life.

Where do I see myself in this area?

1   2   3   4   5

Where do my friends see me in this area?

1   2   3   4   5

Where does my family see me in this area?

1   2   3   4   5

Where do my leaders see me in this area?

1   2   3   4   5

After the assessment, how do you feel? Write a few thoughts below. Share your ideas and/or thoughts and ask for advice, wisdom, and guidance on how to further develop yourself in this area.

"LOVE ALWAYS LEAVES A MARK, AND RELENTLESS PURSUIT IS A DEMONSTRATION OF SELFLESS LOVE."

- THE LOST ART OF DISCIPLESHIP

CHAPTER SIX

RELATIONSHIP

Relational connection will turn a mere church attendee
into a true disciple.

CREATING CONNECTION + INTENTIONALITY + COVERING = RELATIONSHIP

Discipleship rises and falls on **relationship**.

Leaders' influence in the lives of those they lead is proportional to the connection built with them. Connection builds trust—the currency of effective discipleship. Think of it this way: There is a special bond between natural parents and their children. Years of consistent selfless love and investment develops connection over the years because of the trust that is built. In order to invest in spiritual sons and daughters to a similar extent, long-term trust needs to be built, and this comes through intentional displays of love and care. Keeping note of what people appreciate will give you opportunities to express just how much they mean to you. Consistently pursuing relationship with sons and daughters by praying and providing spiritual covering for them will strengthen connection and maximize your opportunity to lead and guide them.

CREATING CONNECTION

Discipleship without *connection* isn't actually discipleship! Close relationships are necessary in the building up of God's Kingdom.

OVERVIEW:

Creating connection is necessary as you begin to pour into the life of a son or daughter.

- The more trust and connection are developed, the more the person you are discipling will be open and comfortable with you.

- Building connection doesn't happen overnight. It takes time, effort, and investment.

- Many people have been hurt by leaders in their past. Don't allow this to offend you or keep you from pursuing relationship with them.

- The more connection people have with their leaders, the more they grow. You should be convinced that when people are around you, they flourish into who God created them to be.

- Prayer develops connection. It allows you to see people with God's eyes and love them with His heart.

- Ask questions to connect on a deeper level.

- Don't forget to have fun!

> "
> AND LET US CONSIDER ONE ANOTHER IN ORDER TO STIR UP LOVE AND GOOD WORKS, NOT FORSAKING THE ASSEMBLING OF OURSELVES TOGETHER, AS IS THE MANNER OF SOME, BUT EXHORTING ONE ANOTHER, AND SO MUCH THE MORE AS YOU SEE THE DAY APPROACHING.
>
> **HEBREWS 10: 24-25**

NOTES:

GOING DEEPER

1. Connection is vital! If you aren't genuinely connected to those you are discipling, that's a sign that it's become more of a job than a relationship. How does your level of connection impact your level of influence in relationships? What kinds of things can you talk about only with those you are very close to?

_____

_____

_____

_____

2. With this in mind, how can you create deeper connections with those you are leading? Pray for ideas of how to intentionally build connection with specific individuals you lead. Write your ideas below.

_____

_____

_____

_____

3. How can you see closer connections affecting the people you disciple? What does it take to develop this kind of connection, and what do you think the result will be over time?

_____

_____

_____

_____

4. Write down the name of someone you'd like to connect with this week. Don't choose someone you're already well acquainted with! Try meeting with someone you don't feel extremely connected to and expect a divine connection to occur. Write the results below.

PRAY IN TONGUES

Prayer brings about unity in ways beyond comprehension. When you view people according to the Spirit and pray for them from that standpoint, your connection will be supernaturally strengthened. God desires us to view everyone in light of what He's accomplished for them. Spend some time praying in tongues! As you pray, think about the people you love and allow God to upgrade your perception of them in a whole new way. Continue until you feel you've received a fresh perspective! "Those who pray together stay together!"

NOTES:

_____

_____

_____

_____

_____

_____

INTENTIONALITY

Love is the driving force of *intentionality*. When your heart is motivated by love, intentionality is a natural byproduct.

OVERVIEW:

Intentionality from a father or mother leaves an impact beyond the surface of relational connection.

- There are no limits to the expression of intentional love.

- Whether big or small, intentional acts of love always make a difference and leave an impact.

- The Cross is the most radical form of intentionality that has ever been displayed, and we have the honor of revealing it to everyone we lead and come in contact with.

- Intentionality is seeing value in another person and demonstrating that value in a creative and meaningful way.

- Even when people don't see their worth, it's important that you consistently reveal it to them in your actions towards them.

- It's not so much about the amount of time spent with someone, but the quality of time spent with them.

- Take note of what your sons and daughters enjoy and use that information to radically bless them.

> "
> A NEW COMMANDMENT I GIVE TO YOU, THAT YOU LOVE ONE ANOTHER; AS I HAVE LOVED YOU, THAT YOU ALSO LOVE ONE ANOTHER.
>
> JOHN 13:34

GOING DEEPER

1. What are three intentional acts you would love to experience from someone? How would it make you feel if someone did these for you?

_____

_____

_____

_____

_____

2. How can you incorporate more intentionality into your family, friends, workplace, or home group? Write down a few ideas! Be creative!

_____

_____

_____

_____

_____

_____

_____

_____

_____

3. Reflect on what Jesus did for you on the Cross. Reflect on His intentionality to die, not only for the sins of the whole world, but for you specifically. He knows the number of hairs on your head and believes every bit of you was worth dying for. How does this make you feel? How can you reciprocate God's love into the lives of others?

4. What do you think will be the long-lasting impact of consistently showing intentionality to those you lead?

♡ MEDITATION

Look back at Psalm 139 and choose a verse that stands out to you. Meditate on it for a few minutes. Picture it and allow it to sink deep into your heart. God's kindness and intentional love towards you is something worth mulling over again and again!

COVERING

When you *cover* someone in love, you give them a place to grow into the man or woman God called them to be.

OVERVIEW:

Beneath the covering of a leader, sons and daughters will rapidly flourish into their God-given potential.

- Discipleship can be likened to a garden—beneath the covering of natural mulch (selfless love), life will quickly emerge.

- The Apostles appointed elders and deacons in the various churches and trusted them to recreate the culture passed on to them.

- The goal of covering is to create an environment where we can help produce in others what has been produced in us.

- Hebrews 11 recounts many men and women who were deemed faithful by God, even though many of them had issues and shortcomings.

- Covering looks different from scenario to scenario, but the goal is always to protect and develop those you are leading.

> "
> 'WHEN I PASSED BY YOU AGAIN AND LOOKED UPON YOU, INDEED YOUR TIME WAS THE TIME OF LOVE; SO I SPREAD MY WING OVER YOU AND COVERED YOUR NAKEDNESS. YES, I SWORE AN OATH TO YOU AND ENTERED INTO A COVENANT WITH YOU, AND YOU BECAME MINE,' SAYS THE LORD GOD.
>
> **EZEKIEL 16:8**

GOING DEEPER

1. Who would you consider to be a covering in your own life? How have they covered you and how has it impacted your life?

2. Take time to read Hebrews 11 and reflect on God's willingness and desire to cover those He loves. How does He present people despite their flaws?

_____

_____

_____

_____

3. How can you take the Hebrews 11 principle and make it practical? If someone makes a mistake, what would it look like for you to cover them?

_____

_____

_____

_____

4. Take time to thank God for His covering over your life and ask Him for His perspective. Let His Word penetrate your heart and awaken you to a new way of seeing! Write down any thoughts or revelations below.

_____

_____

_____

_____

_____

SCAN ME!

THE WORD MADE FLESH

WORD STUDY

Take time to dive into the word and examine from the life of Christ how much He truly loved His disciples. He created connections with them, He was intentional with them, and He covered them. Find three separate passages in the Bible pertaining to each of these to help solidify your value of these components.

_____

_____

_____

_____

_____

_____

(Check the Appendix to see my own findings.)

SELF-ASSESSMENT

Take time to reflect on what your relationships currently look like with those you are leading. Do you feel like you have a strong understanding for creating connection, intentionality, and covering? Or do you feel there's something here you can grow in? No matter where you are at, God's Spirit is ready and waiting to empower you to new heights. God will never put you down, He will only work to transform you and lift you up!

Rate yourself in the respective areas, 1 meaning you really need to work on it, and 5 meaning you are thriving in this area of life.

Where do I see myself in this area?

1   2   3   4   5

Where do my friends see me in this area?

1   2   3   4   5

Where does my family see me in this area?

1   2   3   4   5

Where do my leaders see me in this area?

1   2   3   4   5

After the assessment, how do you feel? Write a few thoughts below. Share your ideas and/or thoughts and ask for advice, wisdom, and guidance on how to further develop yourself in this area.

_____

_____

_____

_____

"IT'S IMPORTANT TO REALIZE THAT IT'S NOT SO MUCH THE QUANTITY OF TIME SPENT, BUT THE QUALITY OF TIME SPENT."

- THE LOST ART OF DISCIPLESHIP

CHAPTER SEVEN

CREATING GROWTH

The words of life and godly wisdom that you pour into your spiritual children will bear no result if they do not open their hearts and say "yes" to the nourishment of the Gospel themselves.

In the midst of every high and low, we can be assured that Christ is daily forming us into His own image. He is constantly revealing a deeper reality of who He is and who we are.

CONFRONTATION + ACTIVATION & EMPOWERMENT + COMMISSIONING = CREATING GROWTH

CREATING GROWTH AT A GLANCE

Like learning to ride a bicycle, growing up is full of hits and misses. It's in the falls that we learn to ride and in the misses that we learn to get better. If a baby never learns to fall, they'll never learn to walk. It's in the process of making mistakes that we mature. It's with this lens that leaders get to view those they are speaking into. Growth can only come when there's correction, and correction can only come when there's failure.

As leaders, we must embrace patience as we, again and again, push our spiritual sons and daughters into new and greater heights. We must look at them through the perfect blood of Christ, daily identifying them with the finished work of the Cross. Before long, we will find them walking in greater maturity, in a position to tackle challenges far bigger than they ever thought they could.

When Jesus commissioned His disciples, He displayed the ultimate goal of investment in others: that they themselves would become living representatives of His message. He created disciples who not only knew Him but also looked like Him. In the same way, we disciple in order to produce leaders who are entirely dependent on the wisdom, strength, and love that already lives within them—Christ Himself.

We develop sons and daughters by giving them opportunities to grow and activating them into their full potential. We guide them along the way, pointing out areas for growth and confronting them as needed. And when they are ready, we commission them into their next phase of life, confident that they will succeed.

CONFRONTATION

> *Confrontation* is nothing more than speaking the truth in love to someone who needs to hear it.

OVERVIEW:

Confrontation leads to growth, transformation, and deeper connection.

- Confrontation is a vital component in being an empowering father or mother.

- The Bible describes confrontation as "life-giving" (see Proverbs 15:31 NIV).

- Punishment lacks love; confrontation is built on it.

- It's important to confront the "little foxes," or small issues, in people's lives.

- Discern the difference between when to have a heavy conversation and when to be more sensitive.

- Confrontation is a call to action and a call to maturity.

- Confrontation allows course correction in the hearts of those we are leading.

- Love never sacrifices the truth; it speaks it boldly.

- Fear, pride, and condemnation are common roots that need to be confronted.

- The goal of confrontation is a transformed heart, fully reliant on Jesus.

> "
>
> **MY SON, HEAR THE INSTRUCTION OF YOUR FATHER, AND DO NOT FORSAKE THE LAW OF YOUR MOTHER.**
>
> **PROVERBS 1:8**

NOTES:

_____

_____

_____

GOING DEEPER

1. List three occasions when something a leader said to you encouraged you to grow beyond your current way of thinking and living. Was it hard at first to hear the truth?

2. What was the fruit of those conversations? Were you glad for them in the end?

3. How can you grow in confronting others? How can you play a more active role in building others up in truth?

_____

_____

_____

_____

4. Name a moment that you said something to someone that wasn't easy to say, but helped them in the end. How did it feel in the moment? Looking back on it, are you glad you spoke up? If you don't have any scenarios like this, make it a goal to speak up more this week!

_____

_____

_____

_____

📢 DECLARATIONS

A lot of times we see things that need to be confronted, but we hold back in fear of what others might think of us. If your tongue has the power to give life, don't you want to use it for that purpose? Confrontation starts with opening your mouth and letting truth flow from your lips with absolute honor and love for the person you are confronting. Practice being bold with your words. Open your mouth and let God's word come out! Make these declarations out loud with boldness. Repeat as many times as you would like.

God has filled me with truth! (See John 16:13.)

My voice needs to be heard because what I have to say is powerful and important. (See Matt. 10:27.)

I see people according to the love that God has for them. (See 2 Cor. 5:14.)

Confrontation is an act of love. (See Prov. 27:6.)

God has put me in people's lives so that iron can sharpen iron! (See Prov. 27:17.)

I am a vessel for God's transformative power, grace, and truth! (See 2 Cor. 4:7.)

NOTES:

ACTIVATION & EMPOWERMENT

Empowerment: authority, right, or power given to someone to do something.

OVERVIEW:

Activation and empowerment cause us to take risks beyond our comfort zone. This leads to accelerated, exponential growth!

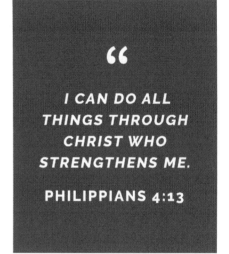

> "
> *I CAN DO ALL THINGS THROUGH CHRIST WHO STRENGTHENS ME.*
>
> **PHILIPPIANS 4:13**

- Activation translates your own growth into the lives of others.

- As leaders, we should desire to awaken people to their full potential.

- Jesus empowered and activated His disciples; we should do the same!

- Don't solve all of your son's and daughter's problems for them! Empower him or her to find the solution.

- You can do *all* things! Think this, speak this, believe this!

- Activation takes place in the context of relational connection. The closer the connection, the greater the empowerment will be.

- Activation takes place in the unknown. When we step out of our comfort zones, we can grow in new ways we never thought possible.

- Put people in situations they have never been in before!

- The more we affirm our sons and daughters in who they truly are, the more they will become those very people.

GOING DEEPER

1. Think of a few basic responsibilities you have on a weekly basis (sending emails, coordinating an event, running errands, etc.) Write them down below.

_____

_____

_____

_____

2. Now, think of a few people you are leading that could help you with these practical tasks. Write their names next to the responsibility you feel they could help you achieve. Reach out to these people and ask them if they'd be willing to help you. Explain to them that you consider them capable and that it would be a good learning experience for them.

_____

_____

_____

_____

3. Take some time to think and pray about the strengths and callings of those you lead. You might be surprised by what you hear! Write them below, and look for opportunities to activate people in those specific areas.

_____

_____

_____

_____

4. Now, what are some ways you could be stretched? What is something you want to do but haven't done yet? Write this below, share what you wrote with someone you look up to, and ask them to spur you on toward doing what you've never done before!

COMMISSIONING

Commissioning is the ultimate display of trust, belief, and empowerment.

OVERVIEW:

Commissioning is an honor for both the giver and the receiver. The giver's vision and mission are expanded with rapid acceleration and the receiver is empowered to thrive at his or her fullest potential.

> **"**
>
> *AND HE SAID TO THEM, 'GO INTO ALL THE WORLD AND PREACH THE GOSPEL TO EVERY CREATURE.'*
>
> **MARK 16:15**

- As fathers and mothers, we have the privilege of commissioning sons and daughters to go beyond our own reach.

- Jesus believed that His physical absence would be filled by His disciples' presence here on Earth.

- We are called to create powerful leaders that are able to recreate what we have deposited into their lives, in the lives of others.

- Through relationship, we should know when our sons and daughters are ready for what's next.

- Use wisdom when deciding when and where to commission your sons and daughters.

GOING DEEPER

1. Read Matthew 28:16-20. What is so significant about Jesus commissioning His disciples? What was He intending for them to do and what did He believe would happen?

_____

_____

_____

_____

2. What would the global impact be if everyone was submitted to and commissioned by spiritual fathers/mothers?

_____

_____

_____

_____

3. How would culture be affected if sons and daughters listened to their leader's words rather than making decisions independent of counsel?

---

4. Are there any people you have been leading that you feel could be sent (either now, or later down the road) to do something beyond what they're currently doing? Ask the Lord and write down what you hear Him saying.

---

5. How can you prepare your son or daughter today to be commissioned into the area, industry, or sphere they are called to in the future? List some core values or strengths that your specific son or daughter needs to be prepared for their area of calling. Next to each attribute, write a few practical things you feel God is leading you to implement for the sake of their growth.

 **MEDITATION**

Read Matthew 28:16-20. Take some time and meditate on being a disciple in this moment. The Son of God is entrusting *you* with the message of salvation. He's commissioning *you* to pick up where He left off. What does it feel like to know that you've been called and empowered to carry the "cure" that all of humanity is waiting for?

_____

_____

_____

_____

_____

_____

_____

_____

SCAN ME!

THE WORD MADE FLESH

WORD STUDY

Read 1 Timothy 4:12-16 and 2 Timothy 2:1-3. What do you examine about Paul's connection with Timothy? In what ways do you see Paul looking beyond himself in order to spread the good news of the Gospel and empower Timothy?

SELF-ASSESSMENT

Take time to reflect on how you are doing with creating growth in the lives of those you are leading. Do you feel like you understand and do well with giving confrontation, activating and empowering, and commissioning? Or do you feel that these are things you can grow in? No matter where you are at, God's Spirit is ready and waiting to empower you to new heights. God will never put you down, He will only work to transform you and lift you up!

Rate yourself in the respective areas, 1 meaning you really need to work on it, and 5 meaning you are thriving in this area of life.

Where do I see myself in this area?

1   2   3   4   5

Where do my friends see me in this area?

1   2   3   4   5

Where does my family see me in this area?

1   2   3   4   5

Where do my leaders see me in this area?

1   2   3   4   5

After the assessment, how do you feel? Write a few thoughts below. Share your ideas and/or thoughts and ask for advice, wisdom, and guidance on how to further develop yourself in this area.

....

....

....

....

"THE ROLE OF A LEADER IS NOT TO GET OTHER PEOPLE TO FOLLOW THEM, BUT TO EMPOWER OTHERS TO LEAD."

- BILL GEORGE

PART THREE

CREATE A CULTURE OF DISCIPLESHIP

You've learned the beauty of positioning yourself as a son or daughter and the power of being a father or mother. Now it's time to learn the joy of being a family.

CREATING FAMILY

The most effective way to build people up in their true identity is by producing a safe environment for them to flourish, fail, and become.

Family brings God's heart and covenant into action. Through unconditional love, we realize we can be ourselves in the good, the bad, and the ugly.

CELEBRATING GROWTH + FAMILY DYNAMIC + VISION, BUY-IN, CULTURE, & PRAYER + COVERING FAILURE + UPHOLDING A STANDARD + RESTORING RELATIONSHIP = CREATING FAMILY

CREATING FAMILY AT A GLANCE

A culture of discipleship is primarily a culture of **family**. A discipleship community is like a grove of Redwood trees. Each tree is distinct and may seem to stand alone, but under the surface, the roots of many trees are all wound together, allowing these extremely tall trees to stay rooted through thousands of storms, some for over 2,000 years. These trees depend on connection with each other to stand. Now that's true family!

Healthy communities spring up when individuals come together and forsake self-reliance. Selfless love builds bonds that stand the test of time, creating family. It's only in the context of family that we can see and encourage deep transformation. When we restore relationships after conflict, cover those we lead, and persist in prayer for everyone in our community, we form relationships that only grow stronger with time. Add to that a common vision among individuals fully committed to the same core values, and you have created a family with its own unique display of Kingdom culture.

SCAN ME!

CELEBRATING GROWTH

Growth is worthy of being celebrated. When you magnify someone's progress you will empower them in their process.

OVERVIEW:

Family should celebrate growth in one another. Hand in hand we carry a common goal: to be conformed into the image and likeness of Jesus Christ.

- Relationships are like bank accounts. Confrontation can feel like a withdrawal. Celebrating growth feels like a deposit.

- When you magnify someone's growth, you fan to flame the embers within them.

- Don't focus on the past! Forget the past, and celebrate what God is doing!

- People are their own worst critics. Further criticism from outside sources will only help to stunt growth, not enhance it.

- Your ability to celebrate your sons' and daughters' growth runs parallel with your ability to believe in them.

- Encouragement is the most practical way to celebrate growth.

- Your words have an impact; speak life!

> "
> AND LET US CONSIDER ONE ANOTHER IN ORDER TO STIR UP LOVE AND GOOD WORKS, NOT FORSAKING THE ASSEMBLING OF OURSELVES TOGETHER, AS IS THE MANNER OF SOME, BUT EXHORTING ONE ANOTHER, AND SO MUCH THE MORE AS YOU SEE THE DAY APPROACHING.
>
> **HEBREWS 10:24-25**

GOING DEEPER

1. Take time to ask a leader to point out areas they've seen you grow in. Go ahead and do it now! Text or call someone you trust and see what they say. Write down his or her response below.

_____

_____

_____

_____

2. How does it feel when people call out your progress? What does it make you want to do?

_____

_____

_____

_____

3. Take time with the Lord and ask Him how He's seen you grow in the past year. Even if things have been rough lately, God always has good things to say about you. Write down what He says below.

_____

_____

_____

_____

_____

4. Now, it's your turn! Reach out to three people this week and encourage them. Let them know you love them and that you see them growing in X, Y, and Z! Record their responses and your experience below.

_____

_____

_____

_____

_____

_____

_____

☑ PRAY IN TONGUES

"For by one Spirit we were all baptized into one body—whether Jews or Greeks, whether slaves or free—and have all been made to drink into one Spirit" (1 Cor. 12:13). As the Body of Christ, we all have one Spirit. It is the Spirit of Christ that knits us together and unites us as one. Spend some time praying in tongues and fix your mind on the reality that your prayers are coming from the same Holy Spirit that dwells within your brothers and sisters in Christ. As you pray, meditate on the unity that we all have simply because we've been born again. Allow God to reveal just how close we are called to be as many members of one body.

NOTES:

_____

_____

_____

_____

_____

_____

HEALTHY COMMUNITY

When a *community* is knit together through the bond of selfless love, the natural byproducts are growth, transformation, and revival.

OVERVIEW:

A healthy community should thrive on selfless love. Selfless love leads us to care for the needs of others, not just ourselves, causing relationships to deepen.

- Family thrives on deep connection and selfless love.

- We cannot grow as a healthy community when we hold onto independence. There is safety, wisdom, and covering within family which guards us from the deceptions of the world that are bred in isolation.

- The fruit that love produces within a family is always worth the sacrifice.

- Being a devoted lover of the Lord doesn't have to look like being a monk! It looks like pouring into others what He has poured into you.

- Humble yourself and seek the interest of others!

- Lay down your guard and be vulnerable within family. Don't be ruled by your emotions, but do invite people into what you are going through and allow them to support you.

- If we remain distant and surface level, true family will never be formed.

- Envision the type of culture you want to create within your community and model it in your daily life.

> "
> BEHOLD, HOW GOOD AND HOW PLEASANT IT IS FOR BRETHREN TO DWELL TOGETHER IN UNITY! IT IS LIKE THE PRECIOUS OIL UPON THE HEAD, RUNNING DOWN ON THE BEARD, THE BEARD OF AARON, RUNNING DOWN ON THE EDGE OF HIS GARMENTS.
>
> PSALM 133:1-2

GOING DEEPER

1. Think of a family you know that is happy, thriving, and well-connected. What do you see them doing that creates such a healthy dynamic?

_____

_____

_____

2. Discipleship is all about family! In your own words, what's the difference between a workplace or organization and a family?

_____

_____

_____

3. How did Jesus build family with His disciples? What are some attitudes or actions of Jesus that you could implement to strengthen your spiritual family?

_____

_____

_____

4. How can you create a true family with those you are connected to? Write down a few intentional things you can do to facilitate and catalyze a healthy community.

_____

_____

_____

_____

5. Start now! Gather your spiritual community (or even your physical family or those from your workplace) and discuss what it would look like to grow closer as a family. Write down how the meeting goes below.

_____

_____

_____

_____

NOTES:

_____

_____

_____

_____

_____

_____

VISION, BUY-IN, CULTURE, & PRAYER

A thriving family is built upon the irreplaceable keys of *vision, buy-in, culture, and prayer.*

OVERVIEW:

Vision, buy-in, culture, & prayer creates a motivated community that stays on course no matter the circumstances or issues surrounding it.

- Your ability to help others see what you see will inspire passion and longevity.

- Buy-in creates a sense of connection as everyone is united to the same vision with their own conviction.

- A leader is like a bus driver. People can ride the bus to where it's going or they can get off at the next bus stop!

- Culture is defined as the "customary beliefs, social forms, and material traits of a racial, religious, or social group."

- A culture is built upon a certain set of core values that are held to with conviction.

- To create and maintain a healthy culture, you must see the importance of investing in people. A shepherd should smell like his sheep. If people are loved and tended to, they will reciprocate that same love within the community.

- Never be too busy to enjoy the relationships God has surrounded you with!

- Make having fun a priority in your community and it will strengthen the connection of everyone involved.

- Those who pray together, stay together. It's in prayer that supernatural bonds are formed!

> "
> I, THEREFORE, THE PRISONER OF THE LORD, BESEECH YOU TO WALK WORTHY OF THE CALLING WITH WHICH YOU WERE CALLED, WITH ALL LOWLINESS AND GENTLENESS, WITH LONGSUFFERING, BEARING WITH ONE ANOTHER IN LOVE, ENDEAVORING TO KEEP THE UNITY OF THE SPIRIT IN THE BOND OF PEACE.
>
> **EPHESIANS 4:1-3**

GOING DEEPER

1. Spend some time in prayer about the vision of your ministry or community. After doing this, compose a vision statement and write it down below. These questions may help: What do you want out of your ministry, organization, or home group? What do you want to happen within your group, and how will it impact the greater community?

For an example, check out the vision statement of Grace Place Ministries:

Mature sons and daughters established in their identity in Christ, spreading the Gospel of grace and truth.

2. What do you notice about the level of buy-in of those in your group, organization, or ministry? Write three practical ways you can impart your vision to those you lead that will cause them to be fully invested in seeing it accomplished.

3. What kind of culture do you want? What do you want your ministry, organization, homegroup to be known for? Dream big!

4. Write down at least three major things you would like to see happen in your community. Share them with your team and spend time in prayer together. Ask them to keep these things in prayer as they go about their daily lives. Use the space below to write the changes and shifts you see as a result. Be patient, and trust that God is working all things together for good (see Romans 8:28)!

NOTES:

COVERING FAILURE

Love *covers* a multitude of sins. It never sees failure as the ultimatum.

OVERVIEW:

Failure should never end relationships. Disciples shoul be given the chance to try and fail and know they are covered.

> "
> AND ABOVE ALL THINGS HAVE FERVENT LOVE FOR ONE ANOTHER, FOR 'LOVE WILL COVER A MULTITUDE OF SINS.'
>
> 1 PETER 4:8

- How we choose to handle failure is more important than failure itself.

- What looks like failure could be your first stepping stone into success.

- When someone fails, they are not projects to be fixed. Put relationship first and look beyond the mess. Look at who God made them to be!

- Peter rejected the Lord three times, yet Jesus never condemned or punished him! He welcomed him back and reminded him of his identity.

- Our failures don't intimidate God.

- People often fall into self-condemnation after making a mistake. They should shake off the condemnation and ask God for conviction. Condemnation leaves us in our mess while conviction empowers us to live at a higher standard by God's grace.

- Use discernment when counseling someone who has failed. If they are believing a lie, don't feed into it! Speak the truth that liberates them from their bondage.

- If people are dealing with genuine pain because of a loss or something similar, be compassionate towards them in the process.

- It's not about the mistake, but how the mistake is cleaned up.

- Forgiveness restores the standard and believes the best.

GOING DEEPER

1. Condemnation is a tactic of the enemy to get us fixated on our failures. It disrupts true intimacy with God. It's a lie that says, "If you feel bad enough about what you've done, you will change." However, it is the love of God that truly transforms us. How do you respond when you come face to face with your failures? Do you withdraw from God when you make a mistake, or do you run to Him? Pray and ask God about this. Write your thoughts and what you feel Him saying below.

2. Forgiveness is more than something we do; it's a way of seeing. Forgiveness is releasing someone from a "judgment" or punishment that you think they deserve. It's a lens we can view the world around us through. What would it look like to not judge anyone according to their sins? Would you behave differently? How would this cause you to treat people?

3. We should always see through the lens of forgiveness. If there are any areas you feel you're harboring unforgiveness in, take time to give it to the Lord! Write down your experience below.

NOTES:

UPHOLDING A STANDARD

In a world of mixed reviews and unsettled opinions, Christ is the shining example for our lives. It should be our ambition to make Jesus' lifestyle our cultural norm.

OVERVIEW:

The standard of character, excellence, and lordship in our lives is found in Jesus Christ Himself. If we lower the standard, sin, compromise, and pride can creep in quickly. Upholding His standard keeps us humble and realizing our need for His grace.

- We are called to live holy lives that are above reproach.

- The values that we live from should not be built on what society dictates or upon our heritage or traditions. In order to walk according to God's standard, we must clear our lens of worldly conduct and put on the ways of the Kingdom.

- When your eyes and your heart are set towards Jesus, living according to His culture and convictions comes easily.

- In order to create a family culture where high standards are sustained, the standards must be modeled by leaders in daily life.

- As believers in Christ, it's our job to change the culture. This is what upholding a standard looks like.

> "
> THEREFORE BE IMITATORS OF GOD AS DEAR CHILDREN. AND WALK IN LOVE, AS CHRIST ALSO HAS LOVED US AND GIVEN HIMSELF FOR US, AN OFFERING AND A SACRIFICE TO GOD FOR A SWEET-SMELLING AROMA.
>
> EPHESIANS 5:1-2

GOING DEEPER

1. How do you see Jesus creating a standard of holiness amongst His disciples?

2. Write down a list of core values you live by that you would like established within your community (ex: purity, a love for the Word of God, generosity).

3. What actions could you personally take to see these values take root in your community?

4. Share these core values with the leaders in your ministry, organization, or home group. Ask them for their thoughts on each one of them and discuss how as a team you could see them established in your culture. Write down the outcome of this discussion below. If you aren't currently in a position of leadership, set up a meeting with someone who is! Ask them about their process in establishing core values within their church, organization, or business, and write what you learn on the lines below.

DECLARATIONS

Take the list of core values that you wrote above and turn them into declarations. For example, if one of your core values is to live in integrity, then make this declaration: "I am a man/woman of integrity! I keep my word and honor those around me!" Use the space below to write out your declarations and then proclaim them with confidence and boldness.

NOTES:

_____

_____

_____

_____

_____

_____

RESTORING RELATIONSHIP

Relationships are worth fighting for. Forgiveness and selfless love restore stifled connection.

OVERVIEW:

Mistakes will happen. Conflicts will occur. Disagreements will be frequent. Don't let it lead to broken relationships—fight for connection and reconciliation!

- We must learn how to work through conflict with one another so that our relational growth may not be stunted.

- In our relationships, we have to choose to believe the best in others even after mistakes have been made. There is never an appropriate time to hold people's past mistakes against them.

- When we walk successfully through conflict together, it creates a bond even deeper than we previously had.

- If a conflict arises, it's important to have a listening ear and a humble heart.

- When being confronted, realize that it's not an attack on who you are. Confrontation is evidence that having a healthy relationship with you is worth fighting for.

> "
> THEN PETER CAME TO HIM AND SAID, 'LORD, HOW OFTEN SHALL MY BROTHER SIN AGAINST ME, AND I FORGIVE HIM? UP TO SEVEN TIMES?' JESUS SAID TO HIM, 'I DO NOT SAY TO YOU, UP TO SEVEN TIMES, BUT UP TO SEVENTY TIMES SEVEN.'
>
> MATTHEW 18:21-22

- Forgiveness is essential in restoring a relationship and resetting the standard.

- We do not forgive because of obligation but through the overflow of what Jesus has done for us. Unforgiveness defiles our hearts but forgiveness preserves our innocence.

- Choosing to restore relationship is the antidote needed to remove any poisons of bitterness that may exist as a result of a conflict.

GOING DEEPER

1. Jesus often implored us to forgive one another. He wanted us to stay connected and to live in peaceful unity! How can you ensure that the people in your community live in forgiveness toward one another?

_____

_____

_____

_____

2. Do any of your relationships need to be restored? If so, ask the Lord what He thinks about the person or people and how you should approach the situation. Write down what He says.

_____

_____

_____

_____

3. Share these core values with the leaders in your ministry/organization/homegroup. Ask them for their thoughts on each one of them and discuss how as a team you could see them established in your culture. Write down the outcome of this discussion below:

_____

_____

_____

_____

THE WORD MADE FLESH

WORD STUDY

Read Colossians 3:12-4:6. Break it down, dissect it, and examine how each of the subjects discussed in this session is written about to the church of Colossae.

When you read this passage, what do you examine about Paul's VISION for the church?

How did he inspire BUY-IN? What would cause them to "board the bus"?

What kind of CULTURE do you see Paul talking about? What kind of environment or atmosphere could you expect to experience walking into the church of Colossae?

What about PRAYER? How did Paul encourage it? What was its purpose?

_____

_____

_____

_____

_____

Spend some time meditating on the type of community Paul was painting a picture of. Chew on this passage regularly. Examine it and see how you can adopt these principles as your own in creating a culture of discipleship.

SELF-ASSESSMENT

Take time to reflect on how you are doing when it comes to creating family. Do you feel like you have a grasp for what it looks like to celebrate growth, build healthy community, uphold a standard, restore relationship, and establish vision, buy-in, culture, and prayer? Or do you feel there are areas you can grow in? No matter where you are at, there is no condemnation! God is always transforming us and never condemning us in our current disposition.

Rate yourself in the respective areas, 1 meaning you really need to work on it, and 5 meaning you are thriving in this area of life.

Where do I see myself in this area?

1   2   3   4   5

Where do my friends see me in this area?

1   2   3   4   5

Where does my family see me in this area?

1   2   3   4   5

Where do my leaders see me in this area?

1   2   3   4   5

After the assessment, how do you feel? Write a few thoughts below. Share your ideas and/or thoughts and ask for advice, wisdom, and guidance on how to further develop yourself in this area.

_____

_____

_____

_____

"WE MUST LEARN TO LIVE TOGETHER AS BROTHERS OR PERISH TOGETHER AS FOOLS."

- MARTIN LUTHER KING JR.

CREATING A CULTURE OF CONFRONTATION

You cannot have healthy community without also having a healthy model for confronting and addressing issues that arise.

Confrontation is key to awakening us to the areas we need to grow in.

DEEPER CONNECTION + THE WHY, WHO, WHAT, & HOW = CREATING A CULTURE OF CONFRONTATION

CREATING A CULTURE OF CONFRONTATION AT A GLANCE

A healthy culture must include a value for direct communication. Speaking the truth in love is vital in family. Otherwise, personal growth will be stunted and relationships will only go so deep. Just as iron sharpens iron, we have the privilege of leading others into greater maturity by fearlessly confronting issues in love as they arise. When we keep the other person's best at the heart of confrontation, we strengthen connection with them in the process of walking through conflict.

DEEPER CONNECTION

A *culture of confrontation* is built upon the pillars of love and truth. When a family is sincere and honest, it thrives and grows.

OVERVIEW:

Don't look at confrontation as the end of the relationship, but the beginning of something deeper.

> "
> MOREOVER IF YOUR BROTHER SINS AGAINST YOU, GO AND TELL HIM HIS FAULT BETWEEN YOU AND HIM ALONE. IF HE HEARS YOU, YOU HAVE GAINED YOUR BROTHER.
>
> MATTHEW 18:15

- Confrontation is a doorway to deeper connection.

- A culture of confrontation is a culture of humility. It demands humility from both the confronter and the confronted.

- Always remember that the motive behind confrontation is love. You are expressing love and value to someone by refusing to let them live with unaddressed error in their life.

- The heartbeat of confrontation is: "It is not about me! It is about this person seeing what they have done and how it has affected others around them."

- It's important to know the "why, who, what, and how" of confrontation.

   - Why do I confront? Where is my heart at in this?
   - Who am I confronting?
   - What am I confronting this person about?
   - How do I confront this person or speak into this situation?

- Humility is key to receiving confrontation. Understand that with every confrontation comes an opportunity for growth.

- It's not about you! It's about the truth being upheld and lives being transformed into the image of Christ.

GOING DEEPER

1. What are the benefits of a culture of confrontation? How would loving accountability affect a community?

_____

_____

_____

_____

2. After coming this far into *The Lost Art of Discipleship,* have any mindsets or ideas about confrontation changed for you? If so, how?

_____

_____

_____

_____

3. How can you implement confrontation into your culture without coming across as controlling or overly authoritative? How can you confront from a heart of total and absolute selfless love? Write out your thoughts.

_____

_____

_____

_____

_____

4. At this point, how well do you feel like you take confrontation? How do you think you can grow?

_____

_____

_____

_____

5. It's important that you don't go looking to take the speck out of your brother's/sister's eye when there is a plank in your own (see Matthew 7:3-5). But what are some areas you feel the Lord has really strengthened and set you free in? Write them down. These are most likely the areas you'll be able to help others see more clearly in.

_____

_____

_____

_____

SCAN ME! 📱

THE WORD MADE FLESH

WORD STUDY

Read the following three passages, keeping in mind that we are the temple of God: Mark 11:15-18, 1 Corinthians 6:19, and Luke 9:51-56. What do you see in the way Jesus confronts? What is His goal? Based on His example, what should our goal be?

SELF-ASSESSMENT

Take time to reflect on where you are at when it comes to creating a culture of confrontation. Do you feel like you have a foundation of deep connection and/or know how to establish it? Or do you feel it's something you can grow in? No matter where you are at, there is no condemnation! God is always transforming us and never condemning us in our current disposition.

Rate yourself in the respective areas, 1 meaning you really need to work on it, and 5 meaning you are thriving in this area of life.

Where do I see myself in this area?

1   2   3   4   5

Where do my friends see me in this area?

1   2   3   4   5

Where does my family see me in this area?

1   2   3   4   5

Where do my leaders see me in this area?

1   2   3   4   5

After the assessment, how do you feel? Write a few thoughts below. Share your ideas and/or thoughts and ask for advice, wisdom, and guidance on how to further develop yourself in this area.

_____

_____

_____

_____

_____

"DON'T RUN AWAY FROM THE PEOPLE THAT HURT YOU. CONFRONT IT AND DEAL WITH IT TODAY."

- ESTHER BECKLEY

CHAPTER TEN

CREATING A CULTURE OF THE SUPERNATURAL

We are made to walk just like Jesus in every respect. We are called to walk in both His character and His power.

RISK-TAKING + THE PROPHETIC + HEALING = CREATING A CULTURE OF THE SUPERNATURAL

CREATING A CULTURE OF THE SUPERNATURAL AT A GLANCE

The supernatural shows we have been born of a whole new nature.

We are different and made for so much more than the world's status quo. We are called to live supernatural lives.

We must keep our focus on Jesus and His power at work in and through us. We must step out, taking Him at His Word. Risk-taking is essential if we are to grow in the supernatural, and it's also the best way to model a supernatural lifestyle and encourage the same in those we lead. What we model, we recreate. Step out in the prophetic and pray for the sick, encouraging those you lead to do the same as they push past fear and learn to follow God.

RISK - TAKING

A culture that encourages taking *risks* is a progressives and life-giving culture.

OVERVIEW:

Risk is faith in action. We are called to exit the borders of our comfort zone in search of something greater!

> **"**
>
> **FOR GOD HAS NOT GIVEN US A SPIRIT OF FEAR, BUT OF POWER AND OF LOVE AND OF A SOUND MIND.**
>
> **2 TIMOTHY 1:7**

- If we truly believe we are called to walk and talk like Jesus, then we should stop at nothing to replicate His miracle-working lifestyle.

- When we have a culture of risk-taking, we are creating the necessary ground for growth to take place. We are preparing a place where Jesus can become the only thing we are dependent on.

- As believers, it is of the utmost importance for us to cling to this truth: with God, all things are possible!

- Faith is spelled T-R-U-S-T. The more you trust in Him, the more you will be propelled to take risks.

- Every day is an opportunity to step out past your comfort zone.

- The possibility, the reach, the limit, of anything or anyone is directly related to the source from where it comes. The moment you awaken to the reality of what your true source is is the moment you will realize what your limits are.

- Courage arises when we renew our minds to the reality of who Christ is within us instead of meditating on our inabilities.

- We limit ourselves because we are coming under the influence of something instead of rising above it. If we want the promised land, we have to get so tired of walking around the wilderness that we push through it.

- Kick fear in the face! Leave your comfort zone, step out, and stretch yourself! Do the impossible!

GOING DEEPER

1. When was the last time you took a risk? It's easy to stay put, but it's beyond the borders of your comfort zone that real transformation takes place!

_____

_____

_____

_____

2. Who are some people (historical, biblical, or even fictional) that chose to live in risk? What character traits do you find they share in common? What was the result of their risk-taking?

_____

_____

_____

_____

3. What is the "riskiest" thing you've ever done? How did you feel afterward?

_____

_____

_____

_____

4. What if our reality was no longer determined by our experience, but rather by what Jesus said is true in His Word? What areas of your life are you settling in that you can surrender to God in order to see His heart, desire, and power on display?

_____

_____

_____

_____

5. Write down a few challenging yet attainable things you want to do, but, for whatever reason, haven't done yet. Circle one and do it THIS WEEK!

_____

_____

_____

_____

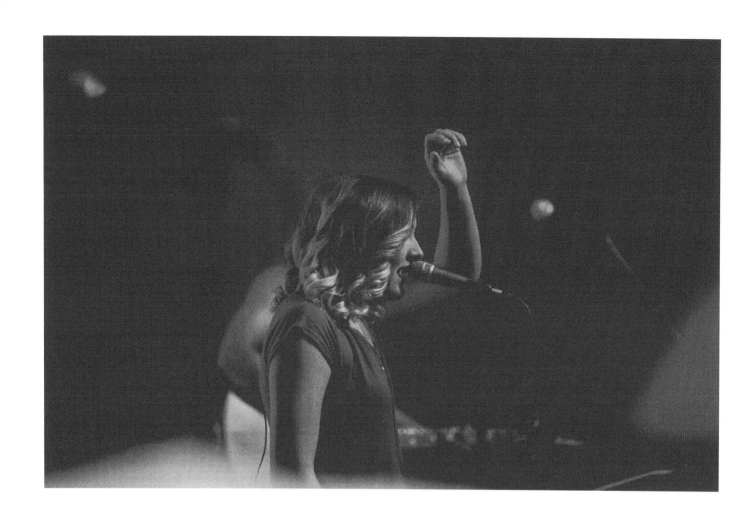

NOTES:

THE PROPHETIC

A *prophetic* culture champions its members into God's reality

OVERVIEW:

Paul says to earnestly desire the spiritual gifts, especially to prophesy. Prophecy is the revelation of God's heart for a person.

> **THEN MOSES SAID TO HIM, 'ARE YOU ZEALOUS FOR MY SAKE? OH, THAT ALL THE LORD'S PEOPLE WERE PROPHETS AND THAT THE LORD WOULD PUT HIS SPIRIT UPON THEM!'**
>
> **NUMBERS 11:29**

- The prophetic is designed to reveal identity and potential in Christ.

- Prophetic words show you the potential that your life has in Christ and allow you to see past any limitations that you may be currently facing.

- Prophetic words instill hope inside of people in order for them to be able to step into their God-given destinies.

- God wants all of us to live in a place with no limitations, restraints, or restrictions!

- A prophetic word over your life always comes with power, and you always have the ability to partner with what has been spoken.

- Take note: if you don't have something good to say about someone, ask God to reveal what He sees in them.

- In order to establish a culture of prophecy in an environment, you must first build a culture of the prophetic within your own heart.

- The more you exercise your "spiritual muscle" of prophecy the more you will grow!

- The goal of the prophetic is to build people up and champion who they are called to be in Christ.

GOING DEEPER

God is always speaking! It may not look like we expect it to, but His voice is constantly reaching out to us.

1. When was the first time you remember hearing God's voice? What did He say? What was it like?

_____

_____

_____

_____

2. Have you ever experienced the voice of God through either giving or receiving a prophetic word? If so, what was it like? How did it make you feel? If you haven't experienced it before, stay tuned for the activation!

_____

_____

_____

_____

3. Do you ever find yourself doubting your ability to walk in the supernatural? Talk to God about relying on His grace. Write below what He says to you.

_____

_____

_____

_____

4. What would it look like to create a culture of the prophetic? How could you implement it into your community?

_____

_____

_____

_____

5. Challenge yourself to prophesy over someone TODAY. If you have experience, prophesy over a stranger. If you don't, prophesy over a friend. It's simple! Ask God one or all of these questions: "What do You think about this person? How do You see them? What person in the Bible do they remind You of and why?" If you are just starting out, it may be helpful to ask for a word first and then ask God who this word is for. Once you hear something, don't hesitate to share it with that person!

_____

_____

_____

_____

NOTES:

_____

_____

_____

_____

_____

HEALING

A culture that leans on God as the ultimate *healer* will thrive in the abundant life Christ came to give us.

OVERVIEW:

When Jesus was whipped and beaten he took every sickness and disease upon Himself. There's no ailment greater than His finished work.

- When the Word of God is preached, miracles, signs, and wonders supernaturally follow.

- God wants you well!

- The same Spirit that was in the disciples is in us today.

- Create an environment of expectancy, where anything is possible!

- Jesus prayed for each individual differently. It's not about a method or formula. It's about doing what the Father is doing.

- It's not so much about the words that you say as it is the authority that you carry.

- Don't beg for God to heal! He wants it more than we do.

- If you're not praying for the sick, it's unlikely that a culture of healing will be created in those that you are leading.

- All Christians are called to pray for the sick.

- Jesus is our permanent standard when it comes to praying for the sick. What He saw, we are made to see!

> "
> HE ALSO BROUGHT THEM OUT WITH SILVER AND GOLD, AND THERE WAS NONE FEEBLE AMONG HIS TRIBES.
>
> PSALM 105:37

GOING DEEPER

1. God wants us to thrive and prosper in every area of our lives. Is there something less than good that you have settled for in an area of your life? Pinpoint whatever that might be and write it down. Now, pray and ask the Lord to reveal His good plans for you, including physical health and wellness. Write what He says.

2. Have you ever seen someone supernaturally healed? If so, what was it like? What happened? If not, stay tuned for the activation!

3. What would it look like to cultivate a culture of supernatural healing and divine health? How could you implement it into your community?

4. Challenge yourself to pray for the sick today. Remember, it's simple! Command the pain, disease, or sickness to go in the name of Jesus. There's no need for a long prayer. Just speak and trust that what Jesus did on the Cross was enough. Be expectant for some incredible miracles!

SCAN ME!

THE WORD MADE FLESH

WORD STUDY

Read Acts 10:37-38. Health and life are from God. Sickness is from the devil. Use the lines below to put your own name in verse 38.

"How God anointed (your name here) of (your city here) with the Holy Spirit and power, and how he/she went around doing good and healing all who were under the power of the devil because God was with him/her."

_____

_____

_____

_____

_____

_____

_____

Make this verse a reality in your life. See yourself doing it. Meditate on what it would be like to walk in the healing power of Jesus Christ, doing good everywhere you go.

SELF-ASSESSMENT

When it comes to creating a culture of the supernatural, where do you see yourself? Do you feel like you encourage and have a value for risk-taking, the prophetic, and healing? Do you see a need for growth in any of these areas? No matter where you are at, there is no condemnation! God is always transforming us and never condemning us in our current disposition.

Rate yourself in the respective areas, 1 meaning you really need to work on it, and 5 meaning you are thriving in this area of life.

Where do I see myself in this area?

1   2   3   4   5

Where do my friends see me in this area?

1   2   3   4   5

Where does my family see me in this area?

1   2   3   4   5

Where do my leaders see me in this area?

1   2   3   4   5

After the assessment, how do you feel? Write a few thoughts below. Share your ideas and/or thoughts and ask for advice, wisdom, and guidance on how to further develop yourself in this area.

_____

_____

_____

_____

"IT'S NOT ABOUT OUR ABILITY AND STRENGTH, BUT IT IS ABOUT HIM WORKING THROUGH US."

- THE LOST ART OF DISCIPLESHIP

CONCLUSION

> **"**
>
> *ARISE, SHINE; FOR YOUR LIGHT HAS COME! AND THE GLORY OF THE LORD IS RISEN UPON YOU. FOR BEHOLD, THE DARKNESS SHALL COVER THE EARTH, AND DEEP DARKNESS THE PEOPLE; BUT THE LORD WILL ARISE OVER YOU, AND HIS GLORY WILL BE SEEN UPON YOU. THE GENTILES SHALL COME TO YOUR LIGHT, AND KINGS TO THE BRIGHTNESS OF YOUR RISING.*
>
> *-ISAIAH 60:1-3*

My hope for you is that The Lost Art of Discipleship would no longer be "lost" in the unknown, but simply waiting.

It's waiting for someone like you, who has positioned themself for greatness; someone who is ready to see God's Kingdom invade the earth, who is burning to see revival, and who is willing to accept a father or mother's correction as a means to do so.

My prayer is that you would position yourself as a son/daughter, lead as a father/mother, and create a culture of discipleship.

Daniel Timothy Newton

FINAL QUESTIONS & REFLECTIONS

1. Take some time to reflect on your journey through *The Lost Art of Discipleship*. What are some of the biggest things you've learned?

_____

_____

_____

_____

_____

_____

_____

2. What are some of the greatest challenges you faced and overcame?

_____

_____

_____

_____

_____

_____

_____

3. Which section was the most impactful for you? What made it so?

4. Which topics do you feel the most equipped to teach?

5. How can you ensure that what you learned doesn't end in yourself but continues into the lives of those around you?

THE WORD MADE FLESH

BIBLE STUDY

Read Habakkuk 2:14. Take time to meditate on the reality of this Scripture. What will it look like for the knowledge of His glory to fill the earth, to fill His people? What will it look like when His nature becomes so apparent and so bright in His sons and daughters all across the world? What will it look like for the knowledge of His glory to fill *you*?

_____

_____

_____

_____

_____

_____

_____

APPENDIX

When organizing this workbook,

I knew it would be used by individuals and leaders alike. My ultimate goal for *The Lost Art of Discipleship Workbook* is for it to be used in tandem with the full curriculum in group settings. I added this appendix including additional activations and discussion questions for this purpose. While it's important to spend time on each topic as an individual, it's equally important to rub elbows with a group of like-minded believers who are also on the same journey of growing in Christ-likeness. I encourage readers to find (or start!) a discipleship group with like-minded believers who are passionate to grow together in Christ.

GROUP QUESTIONS

These questions are to facilitate group discussion in a home group or group study setting. Designed to equip leaders with prompts to guide conversation as well as for group members to reference, use these questions to initiate a dialogue about the topic at hand. However, once the meeting starts, be ready to follow the Holy Spirit as He takes over and personalizes each conversation to each particular meeting. In addition, you may wish to take time to answer these questions yourself beforehand and supplement them with some of your own.

ACTIVATIONS

I've also included additional activities to inspire group members to implement what they are learning into their daily life. These disciplines include both those that can be completed during a group meeting and those that group members can do during the week. They are geared to be optional supplements to the "Going Deeper" questions in the main text of this workbook. Leaders are encouraged to ask group members to share their experiences with these activities as well as what other ways God is encouraging them to grow in each topic.

GROUP QUESTIONS

PART ONE: Position yourself as a Son/Daughter

CHAPTER ONE : Discipleship at its Roots

1. What do you hope will be different in your life as a result of completing The Lost Art of Discipleship?

2. Do you feel that discipleship comes naturally to you? Do you find it easier to be a "Timothy," a "Barnabas," or a "Paul?"

3. Who are those in your life that you already have a discipleship relationship with?

CHAPTER TWO : Humility

SURRENDER

1. Discuss your experience going through the individual questions. What did God show you? What did you learn? How were you challenged?

2. What is your concept of discipleship, and what experiences have led to your current understanding?

3. How do you feel about this statement: "Trusting leaders is ultimately a reflection of the choice to trust God"? Discuss this as a group.

4. Take time to pray together, asking God to lead you as a group and as individuals as you read this book and go through this workbook. Ask Him what He plans to teach you, and write down any thoughts or feelings you have.

SUBMISSION

1. In a few sentences, what is God's design for discipleship as displayed by Jesus in the Word of God?

2. What qualities are in the life of a healthy spiritual son/daughter? How should a spiritual son/daughter view a spiritual father/mother?

3. What do you hope to learn as you submit to and honor fathers and mothers in your life? What will this look like practically? How do you begin?

4. Is there any hesitancy in you as you begin this journey of discipleship? Discuss this within your group, and take time to ask any questions you may have.

CHAPTER THREE : Relationship

PURSUING LEADERSHIP

1. What are the characteristics of a healthy spiritual father or mother? How do you identify one?

2. How do we know who to pursue as spiritual fathers and mothers? Have you had any experience with this, and if so, what was it?

3. What does it look like to pursue leaders as individuals? How can you grow in connection with leaders so that you can pursue them with a greater level of intentionality?

4. Who in your life has the characteristics of a healthy spiritual father or mother? What would it look like to pursue relationship with this person?

INTENTIONALITY

1. How does intentionality display God's heart of love for people? When was Jesus intentional with His disciples?

2. Leaders go out of their way to be intentional with those they lead. What are small, everyday expressions of intentionality you can show to display gratitude and build relationship?

3. Split the group into pairs or groups of three. Ask yourself the following questions about your partner(s), and write down the answers that come to mind (don't share with your partner(s) until the end). You may not know the answers, and that's okay! See this as an opportunity to get to know someone intentionally.

    a. Three things they appeciate
    b. Their favorite
        i. Meal and drink
        ii. Sport, flower, or TV show
    c. Something that makes them cringe
    d. A favorite childhood memory they have

Now share your answers with your partner. Tell each other the real answers, and take note of what your partner says!

Take time to compile a list of these facts and more about the people you seek to build relationship with. Pay attention to what things the leaders in your life value and appreciate, and keep note of them so you can intentionally pursue them.

SERVANTHOOD

1. What would the world look like if everyone were looking out for the interests of others rather than their own? Describe a world filled with selfless love and intentional acts of service.

2. Is it possible to take servanthood too far? What is the ideal heart posture to serve from?

3. Oftentimes, servants are not acknowledged for what they do. What would it look like to continue serving in your current position without recognition or promotion?

4. Jesus was the perfect model of a servant. What qualities can you learn about servanthood from His example? When did He display these?

CHAPTER FOUR : Growth

CONFRONTATION

1. What core values/character aspects that we've explored in our journey of *The Lost Art of Discipleship* will help you receive confrontation well?

2. How is receiving correction and confrontation a fruit of submission?

3. How do you feel when someone points out areas in which you can grow? What is your typical reaction?

4. How can you respond in humility even when you don't agree with how or why a person confronts you? How do you handle this situation?

INTEGRITY

1. Why is it so important to live in integrity in the little things of life? What can you do today to strengthen your integrity?

2. The foundation for integrity is a "sound mind" (see 2 Tim. 1:7, Rom. 12:2, Rom. 8:6). How can we develop a disciplined thought life?

3. What is the "conscience"? Can you recall any times you heard it speak but did not follow it? What was that experience like?

4. Where do we find the strength to live with integrity in every moment? What is our motivation?

RESPONSIBILITY

1. What are areas in your life or projects assigned to you that you've managed responsibly? What was the fruit, and how did it impact those around you?

2. How can we practically grow in responsibility in our day-to-day lives? Brainstorm a few practical actions you can take or any mindsets you can shift to grow in how you steward what's given to you.

3. What (do you think is) is a healthy heart motivation for a son or daughter who's been given more responsibility? How can we handle increased responsibility with maturity and humility?

4. At what point do you realize that you have too much on your plate so you need to look to others to help? Where do you draw the line between lacking responsibility and taking ownership?

PART TWO: Lead as a Father/Mother

CHAPTER FIVE : Love

BELIEF

1. Have you felt God leading you to step up as a father or mother in the life of someone you're leading? What has that looked like?

2. What is your vision for the next generation? What part do you want to play in seeing them get there?

3. What does it feel like to be believed in? Who is someone who has believed in you and how did it affect you?

4. What do you think would happen if someone believed in you even when you didn't believe in yourself? How would that change the way you live?

5. Now, how can you take this information and make a difference in another's life by expressing your belief in them?

SERVANTHOOD

1. How did Jesus model servanthood? What was His model of servant leadership?

2. What is the ideal motive for servanthood? What does this look like practically?

3. Consider the power of leading by example. How do you think modeling servanthood will lead to a value for serving in those you lead?

4. What can you do this month to serve your community/church in a big way? Brainstorm as a group one way you can serve and put it into action!

CHAPTER SIX : Relationship

CREATING CONNECTION

1. How would you invest in relationship with someone if you knew you would be closely connected to them for the rest of your life?

2. What are some signs that your discipleship relationship lacks friendly connection?

3. How do you foster connection without forming unhealthy familiarity with those you lead?

4. What is the balance in "leaders first, friends second"? Does it differ depending on the relationship? If yes, how so?

INTENTIONALITY

1. Take out the notes you made while going through Session 4 of the workbook. What have you added to your note? Have you seen this tool help express intentionality in relationships? Share your experience.

2. What are some specific ways you could be intentional with those you lead?

3. How do you build relationship with someone you feel God is leading you to invest in but isn't positioned to you as a son/daughter? What role could intentionality play in this?

COVERING

1. How does covering encourage growth?

2. What does it mean to see someone not according to the flesh, but according to Christ?

3. How do you balance covering someone you lead with letting them face the consequences of their mistakes? Talk through specific situations and discuss how to cover and teach your sons and daughters when they make mistakes.

4. How would you navigate covering your son/daughter for a situation that you were not present for?

CHAPTER SEVEN : Creating Growth

CONFRONTATION

1. Be honest—where are you at with this topic? What feelings arise when you hear the word "confrontation"?

2. It is best to learn how to confront people in little things so that you are prepared in bigger situations. How will you grow in this skill of confrontation? What will your response be the next time you find yourself in a situation where you can confront another person?

3. How do you confront someone to address a root issue instead of only addressing the more superficial action?

4. What does it look like to confront with a motivation of selfless love instead of criticism?

ACTIVATION & EMPOWERMENT

1. How can you cover and love someone while empowering them to do something outside their comfort zone?

2. How do you know when someone is ready to be activated and empowered? What are some things you can look for?

3. How can you support those you've activated when they are struggling without "taking the wheel" for them?

4. How can you create an atmosphere of trust where those you lead feel comfortable when activated? What values are important in forming this trust?

COMMISSIONING

1. Discuss the power of prayer when it comes to commissioning those you lead. Do you find it challenging to hear what God is saying about your specific sons/daughters' callings?

2. How do you know when a son/daughter is ready to be commissioned? What factor does his/her input have in this? What are some things to keep in mind when considering whether or not someone is ready to be commissioned? (For reference, see the list of questions on pages 106,107)

3. Consider if someone you were leading was set on making a "good" decision you thought they were not ready for. What would you tell them?

4. What would you do if someone you were leading settled for something smaller than their true potential?

PART THREE: Create a Culture of Discipleship

CHAPTER EIGHT : Creating Family

CELEBRATING GROWTH

1. What is your role as a leader to motivate those you lead? How can you be more effective in this?

2. How can you intentionally focus on growth that is already happening while pointing out areas in which growth is necessary?

3. How can we train ourselves to see growth in others?

4. How would you encourage someone who is very fixated on negative things in their past?

HEALTHY COMMUNITY

1. What has your journey with family been like? Do you find that God has redefined your perspective of family? If so, how?

2. What does it look like to preserve family even in the midst of conflict? How can you navigate conflict together so well that it brings you closer rather than tearing you apart?

3. How do you know who your "family" is? What are some signs that God might be leading you to especially invest in certain relationships?

4. How do you navigate managing your time alone and your time with family? What are some indicators that might tell you if you have become unbalanced in this area?

VISION, BUY-IN, CULTURE, & PRAYER

1. How do you inspire vision in those you lead? What are some indicators that those you lead need more vision, personally or corporately?

2. How do you measure how effectively you are accomplishing your vision?

3. What is the most effective way to transfer culture into those you lead? How can you be more intentional in influencing those around you, and what role does confrontation play in this?

4. What makes you want to buy in to something? How can you facilitate this same desire within those you are leading?

5. Do you prioritize having fun highly enough? What are some benefits of having fun as a group other than strengthened connection?

COVERING FAILURE

1. How do you cover someone's mistake without condoning his/her behavior?

2. Do you notice feelings of condemnation affecting you or those you lead? How does one combat condemnation so that mistakes propel us forward instead of holding us back?

3. How can you create a value for forgiveness in those you lead?

4. How can you create an environment that focuses on forgiveness rather than sin? What are some things you could share or teach that would help create a culture of mercy and grace?

UPHOLDING A STANDARD

1. What factors are significant when determining cultural standards of behavior?

2. What standards did Jesus model for us, and how can we establish culture in alignment with them?

3. How would you lead someone into maturity who has a low standard of cultural acceptance?

4. How do you model a standard to those you lead? Is there a place for teaching a standard as well?

RESTORING RELATIONSHIP

1. How do you approach rebuilding a relationship that has been dismantled for some time? What are some factors to consider?

2. Is forgiveness a journey or a one-time decision?

3. What does it mean to believe the best about someone even after they've disappointed you or done something that created distance in your relationship?

4. Relationships must be maintained consistently to prevent distance from creeping in. What are some indicators that a relationship may need more investment?

CHAPTER NINE : Creating a Culture of Confrontation

DEEPER CONNECTION

1. Where do you draw the line between too much confrontation and not enough?

2. Someone you are leading comes to you presenting an issue that arose with a friend you do not know. How would you handle the situation you were not present for?

3. SCENARIO TRAINING: It's time to role-play some situations where confrontation is necessary! Choose someone who will be Billy/Becky and someone else who will be Rick/Rachel. Finally, choose someone who will be Collin/Colleen the Righteous Confronter! Have the first two people engage in an absurd and creative conflict between one another. Then, have the confronter come in and bring truth, life, and clarity to the situation. Have fun, but be real! Play out the scenario and practice your confrontation skills.

4. Mix up the scenarios and do this a few times over. Make sure everyone gets a chance to be Collin/Colleen the Righteous Confronter!

5. Discuss what you learn after each scenario.

CHAPTER TEN : Creating a Culture of the Supernatural

RISK-TAKING

1. What benefits do you think would come from living a life of risk?

2. What does it look like to depend on Christ's strength within you when taking risks?

3. How can you help those you lead step past fear? How can you communicate that fear is holding them back?

4. How can you ensure that risk-taking becomes a lifestyle that you adopt?

THE PROPHETIC

1. Is your community experienced in hearing the voice of the Lord in everyday life? If not, lead a group activation and/or discuss together ways to activate those you lead in basic exercises to hear God's voice, such as asking Him for a Scripture verse in response to specific questions you have. If your community is more experienced, how can you take your group to the next level?

2. Do you feel there is any danger in the prophetic? How can you safely shepherd those you lead to grow in this area by taking risks?

3. What role does faith play in people reaching their God-given destinies? How can prophetic words strengthen faith?

4. Proverbs 18:21 says that "life and death are in the power of the tongue." Discuss the power and potential of creating a prophetic culture.

HEALING

1. What does it mean to have authority in Christ? What has He given us in giving His Spirit?

2. Living a supernatural life is primarily about following the Holy Spirit. What does it look like to listen to and follow the leading of the Holy Spirit while ministering? What are some ways to activate those you lead in this?

3. We do the supernatural because we serve a supernatural God and are one with His supernatural Spirit. We must believe this as the Body of Christ if we are to see healing and miracles in our lives! What role does expectation play in seeing the supernatural come through your hands?

4. How can we renew our minds (and the minds of those we lead) to instantly think of praying for healing when we find out someone is sick?

ACTIVATIONS

PART ONE: Position yourself as a Son/Daughter

CHAPTER ONE : Discipleship

1. Take time to pray and write out a list of leaders you admire (anyone, whether you know them personally or not).

- Beneath each name, list the characteristics and qualities they have that you would like to walk in.
- Circle the most important characteristics for you to grow in right now.
- Which leaders in your life are strongest in the areas of your current growth objectives?

2. Take a step and reach out to a leader in your life right now.

- Text, call, or ask them how you can be praying for them.
- See how you might be able to connect more in the future.
- Request a one-on-one meeting this week.

CHAPTER TWO : Humility

1. This week, take some time to have an out-loud conversation with God. Get away from the noise, whether that looks like a prayer walk or some time alone in your room. Talk to Him plainly like you would a role model or leader you trust. (Use the areas you wrote about in the "Going Deeper" section of this chapter.) Open your heart to the Lord and share your dreams with Him. Allow yourself to trust Him without being held back, and hear what He has to say about your deepest desires. Now take those dreams from your heart and place them into His hands. Trust Him with those vulnerable desires, and trust that He and He alone will lead you into the perfect plan for your life.

2. Go tell someone you trust about the different areas you had to surrender.

3. Look for areas you have in your life where you struggle to agree with others. Take some time to identify if there is any lack of humility towards this area or perhaps a certain individual. Are there any scenarios that come to mind where you refused another person's input in your life because you were hard-hearted or prideful? Reach out to that individual and do your part to reconcile where you failed to receive their correction.

4. Consider the authority figures God has placed in your life, including teachers, pastors, bosses, coaches, or mentors. Which do you struggle most to listen to and receive input from? Deliberately set a timer and pray for them, their family, their work, and for the Lord to increase and bless every area of their life.

5. If you have any disconnection or fracture in the relationship, reach out to them, humble yourself, and apologize for any ways you have dishonored, disrespected, or failed to submit to their leadership. Even if a particular leader may have many areas that he or she needs to grow in, recognize that there is still something you can learn from them if you position yourself in humility.

CHAPTER THREE : Relationship

1. Take some time and write down several questions you have for your leader/mentor. (These questions can be about anything - Scripture, life, issues, goals, etc.) During your next meeting, ask these questions.

2. Go out of your way to find a way to serve a leader in your life. Ask them how they need help or if there is anything you could do to make their life easier.

3. Hand-write a letter to a leader thanking them for how they have invested in you and those around you.

CHAPTER FOUR : Growth

1. Think of "a mess" you've made recently with someone in your life. If you haven't apologized yet, take some time to go through "The 5 A's of Cleaning up a Mess" (on page 49) with them. Recognize that you will only be able to develop the healthy relationship you are wanting after first "cleaning up your mess."

2. Take a look at the responsibilities that you have, and pick 1 or 2 that no one else would be able to tell if you accomplished properly or not. Go out of your way to make sure you handle those with the most excellence, developing a drive for integrity in your life.

3. Pick an area that you would like to steward better or something you have demonstrated a lack of responsibility for. Think of a leader in your life who is successful in this area. Ask them for advice on how to better steward this responsibility and for their covering and accountability.

4. Ask close family, friends, and leaders what they think your top 3 strengths are. If possible, ask them to share with you in person or by video call so you can hear from them face-to-face.

PART TWO: Lead as a Father/Mother

CHAPTER FIVE : Love

1. Set aside time to pray for each person you are leading, intentionally asking God to reveal how He sees them. Write out the following as you hear from Him:

- How He sees them
- Their strengths and spiritual giftings
- His vision for their current season
- Why He has put you specifically in their life
- Gifts and strengths you have that they will learn through your leadership
- Strategies for how to love them well

2. Send a voice message or video to someone you believe in, calling out the strengths you see in them and the potential they have. This can be especially meaningful in an area they may have insecurity in.

3. Let your actions speak louder than your words! Anonymously bless someone by removing a burden from their day or giving them a gift.

CHAPTER SIX : Relationship

1. Spend time with the people you're leading this week. Don't be afraid to have fun with them. (Find out what they enjoy doing. Maybe it's outdoor activities or watching movies, etc.) Remember, you don't have to make it overly "spiritual." Trust the process of building relationships organically with them. Ask them questions to get to know them better.

2. Oftentimes, people assume that a leader will only invest in them during a church activity. But the power of true discipleship is being involved in the day-to-day lives of those you lead. Take time to send an encouraging text message to those you are leading this week. Ask them how they are doing and if there is anything you can pray for them for.

3. Purchase a small gift or snack (doesn't need to be expensive) that you know those you lead will specifically appreciate. This will show them how intimately and uniquely you know them and it will be a delightful and unexpected blessing in their day.

4. It is important for those you are leading to feel safe around you, whether that be in taking risks to challenge themselves to grow or in sharing intimate/vulnerable things about what they are struggling with. What is something one of the people you are leading is pursuing growth in right now? Provide covering by helping them accomplish their goals. If they fail, actively show them you love them by helping them through it.

The Word Made Flesh - Bible Study (Pg. 91)

Jesus created connection with His disciples -- He ate and drank with them (John 13:23). He was intentional -- when Peter needed to pay taxes he told him to go fishing (Peter's profession) to find what he needed (Matthew 17:27). He covered--when people accused His disciples of breaking Sabbath he covered them (Mark 2:23-27).

CHAPTER SEVEN : Creating Growth

1. Get with a friend and practice some mock confrontation scenarios so you can get used to this type of conversation. Feel free to have some fun with these, and deal with issues like, "My roommate doesn't clean up after themselves." "Your friend has an unhealthy addiction to milk." "Someone you are leading cusses casually."

2. Have you noticed that someone you are leading (who has become like a son or daughter to you) could be given an opportunity to grow through serving? The next time you have an important task, reach out to this person and ask if they would be interested in helping you. This gives them the opportunity to learn and grow through serving, and it allows you to spend more quality time with them in the midst of your ordinary life.

3. Are there any connections or relationships you have with other leaders that you can introduce your son/daughter to? Show your belief in their readiness to "be sent" by connecting them with someone who will empower their potential.

PART THREE: Create a Culture of Discipleship

CHAPTER EIGHT : Creating Family

1. Identify areas of weakness that those in your community are actively growing in. To show them you recognize where they've grown, write intentional sticky notes to place in an area they will see them, or send them a text message or letter.

2. Publicly acknowledge someone in an area they are not typically celebrated in so others can see and appreciate it too.

3. Pick a tradition or common practice from your family life that you value and find a way to introduce it in your community. Explain its significance to you. Use the time to enjoy connecting with others in an out-of-the-box way (such as cooking a unique family dinner, celebrating a holiday, etc).

4. Find someone within your community who is living intentionally (demonstrating high buy-in and motivation). Ask this person if there is anything they have been dreaming about, wanting to start, or eager to have others participate in. See if you can join him or her in this endeavor and help make it a reality, even helping rally others to add fuel to their fire!

5. Brainstorm a redemptive way to connect with someone who has failed or made a mess in your community. Reach out to them and connect with them in a way that lets them know you love them in the midst of their failure, not just despite it.

6. Practice consistency in your confrontation and lifestyle. See if there are areas where you have not been living the standard you had envisioned for the culture around you. Publicly apologize to those who have been affected and recommit to holding yourself and others to that standard.

CHAPTER NINE : Creating a Culture of Confrontation

1. Together with others that are growing in discipleship, practice some more role-play scenarios. (Here are some examples of issues to confront: Someone you are leading has lied to you, compromised in their purity, or was very disrespectful and prideful towards you.) Taking turns, give feedback to the other person as you act out the scenarios. As you are watching a scenario, ask: Are they communicating in love? Did they communicate clearly and directly? If not, how could this person be more balanced in their approach?

CHAPTER TEN : Creating a Culture of the Supernatural

1. Spend some time in the presence of God. Start by worshiping, speaking in tongues, or meditating. Become aware of His goodness all around and within you. Allow the supernatural God to touch your heart in a supernatural way. Ask to feel Him, hear Him, and experience Him in a way that you never have before. You are now on your way to creating a culture of the supernatural! The miracles of Jesus stemmed from the overflow of His union with God, knowing He was the Father's Beloved. This is a beautiful model for each of our lives.

2. Take a moment to record or write out a prayer and prophetic word for three different people in your life that you would like to encourage. Choose one person that you know well, one person who you know is in need of encouragement, and one person you don't know very well yet. If you are actively discipling people in your life, encourage them to do the same and debrief how they felt this went.

3. Does something look scary? THEN DO IT! The next time you feel uncomfortable about handling a situation, decide to step out in faith instead of overthinking it. To kick things off, plan a day with your group to do some street evangelism or to pray for anyone you know of who may be sick within your community. If you are actively discipling sons and daughters, ask them if there are areas like this they would like to step out in, and plan an outing or prayer meeting together with them.

ADDITIONAL RESOURCES

THE LOST ART OF DISCIPLESHIP
Online Course

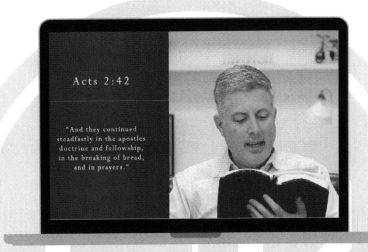

You can live the Great Commission. Every believer is called to embrace Jesus' final command: to make disciples... and this interactive online course is designed to take you even deeper into the rich content taught in *The Lost Art of Discipleship*.

Whether you are wanting to position yourself as a son or daughter, lead as a father or mother, or create a culture of discipleship, this course is for you! Rediscover the lost art with over five hours of video content, practical teaching, quizzes, and supernatural activations from Daniel Newton.

Access and enroll at GracePlaceMedia.com

@GracePlaceDiscipleship

ADDITIONAL RESOURCES

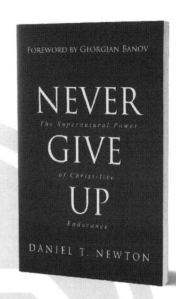

TRUTH IN TENSION
55 Days to Living in Balance

NEVER GIVE UP
The Supernatural Power of Christ-like Endurance

Other Titles

THE LOST ART OF PERSEVERANCE
Rediscover God's Perspective on Your Trials

IT IS FINISHED (COMING SOON)
Exposing the Conquered Giants of
Fear, Pride, and Condemnation

ALL THINGS (COMING SOON)
Beholding Christ's Limitless Work

Available at GracePlaceMedia.com

@GracePlaceDiscipleship

ADDITIONAL RESOURCES

IMMEASURABLE
REVIEWING THE GOODNESS OF GOD

You are made in the image of the Miracle Worker, designed to manifest His glorious nature. Immeasurable: Reviewing the Goodness of God is a collection of 100 real-life stories of salvation, healing, deliverance, signs and wonders, reconciliation, and provision. Every miracle is a prophetic declaration of what God wants to do in, through, and for someone just like you.

Available at GracePlaceMedia.com

@GracePlaceDiscipleship

ADDITIONAL RESOURCES

GP MUSIC: BEGINNINGS

Grace Place Ministries'
Debut Worship Album

Everyone has a story. Most people don't realize that God doesn't just want to improve their story. He wants to rewrite it. Beginnings offers a fresh start, a new focus. This worship album invites you into the core anthems of grace and truth which have impacted us at Grace Place.

Our prayer is that this album helps you lay down your past mistakes, your present circumstances, and your future worries in order to lift both hands high in surrender to the One you were created to worship. We ask that you join us in a new beginning—an exciting start to a life filled with perseverance, focus, and surrender.

Available on all music platforms
or at GracePlaceMedia.com

@GracePlaceDiscipleship

Made in the USA
Columbia, SC
11 February 2022